LANGUAGE AND STYLE SERIES
General Editor: STEPHEN ULLMANN

II

SEYMOUR CHATMAN

THE LATER STYLE
OF HENRY JAMES

NEW YORK
BARNES & NOBLE, INC.
1972

© Basil Blackwell 1972

First published in the United States, 1972
by Barnes & Noble, Inc.
New York, New York

ISBN 389-04481-4

Printed in Great Britain

CONTENTS

BOTH of the following sentences profess to be parodies of the later Jamesian style. Which is better? Which more accurately strikes the Jamesian 'note'?

It might almost perhaps have been one of those strangely if artistically and impressively carved figures of stone, basalt one would say or granite, for the colour varied from gray-brown to a reddish as of gingerbread, which one may come upon in the forests of Mexico, where the Aztecs used to, so at least I gather from history, congregate about their rock-hewn altars to propitiate some polysyllabic deity; for he stood as if petrified by some superhuman power, immovable as the Matterhorn, like a person without an alternative, immersed in immobility up to his chin.

That it hardly was, that it all bleakly and unbeguilingly *wasn't* for 'the likes' of *him*—poor decent Stamfordham—to rap out queries about the owner of the to him unknown and unsuggestive name that had, in these days, been thrust on him with such a wealth of commendatory gesture, was precisely what now, as he took, with his prepared list of New Year *colifichets* and whatever, his way to the great gaudy palace, fairly flicked his cheek with the sense of his having never before so let himself in, as he ruefully phrased it, without letting anything, by the same token, out.

Most readers of James, I think, would choose the latter. The grounds for doing so, however, might seem less clear than the choice itself, more a question of feeling than of method. But stylistic intuitions can be documented, and stylistic features defined. There is no particular reason for assuming that the elements of James' style are less definable than those of other writers. My purpose is to describe those elements, and my success or failure may be judged by my ability to account for the success or failure of these parodies, which I shall attempt to do in the last section of this book.

1. 'ABSTRACT', 'GENERAL', 'INTANGIBLE'

I start with the usual characterization of James' later style as 'difficult'.[1] Doubtless many features—'those notorious idiosyncrasies'—can be seen most clearly in that light. But surely 'difficulty' is a consequence, not a formative principle or 'motive' of a style ('motive' in the sense of 'constitutive element', to avoid any discussion of authorial intention or biographical source; aesthetic, functional intention; what the *work*, not the author, 'intends').[2] One of the causes of difficulty is said to be James' *abstractness*: 'it is commonly recognized that the reading of the later works of Henry James is an exacting task, and at least one explanation of the difficulty that has sometimes been suggested (but not pursued beyond the suggestion) is that it is due to a certain baffling *abstractness*.'[3] The effect of abstractness probably cannot be dissociated from others that arise in the reading of James, in particular a distinctive kind of vague allusiveness, usually the product of extensive and radical ellipsis. This and other features will be

---

[1] My debt to earlier studies will be obvious, particularly to Vernon Lee (Viola Paget), *The Handling of Words* (London, 1923), pp. 241–51; R. W. Short, 'The Sentence Structure of Henry James', *American Literature*, XVIII (1946), pp. 71–88; Dorothea Krook, 'The Method of the Later Works of Henry James', *London Magazine*, I (1954), pp. 55–70; and Ian Watt, 'The First Paragraph of *The Ambassadors*: An Explication', *Essays in Criticism*, X (1960), pp. 250–74.

[2] And 'intends' in the sense of 'requires', not 'wants' or 'attempts'.

[3] Krook, p. 55. (Is it 'the abstractness is of a baffling kind' or 'It is baffling that James should have elected to be so abstract'?) In her book, entitled *The Ordeal of Henry James* (Cambridge, 1962), Miss Krook reprints this article, in slightly revised form, as an appendix. One of the revisions is to change 'abstract' to 'general', but elsewhere (p. 198) she equated the two terms.

mentioned in passing, as causes of further complications for the reader. But the main topic of this study is James' abstractness.

Any inquiry into topics like abstractness, vagueness, allusiveness, and complexity must of course search for detailed causes in the author's language. As Stephen Ullmann has pointed out clearly in 'New Bearings in Stylistics', stylistics can proceed either from Outward Form to Inner Meaning (O→I) or from Inner Meaning to Outward Form (I→O). One can start with a specific stylistic feature and investigate its effect; or, conversely, go from the effect to 'the devices available for producing it'.[1] My concern is the latter: to describe the devices or choices—syntactic and lexical—that evoke the 'specific effect' of abstractness in the reading of James.

First the term itself, and it is not an easy one. A most useful account of the word has been given by W. K. Wimsatt,[2] who points out that there is not one but three dichotomies to consider: 'general' vs. 'particular' (or, better, 'specific'), 'abstract' vs. 'concrete', and 'sensory' vs. 'non-sensory'. These tend to overlap, but theoretically they are clear enough. Generality/specificity is a hierarchical relationship based on a principle of inclusion, as is clear from the cognates 'genus'/'species'. 'Horse' is more general than 'stallion', 'stallion' more specific than 'horse'; 'stallion' is a species of (included in) the genus 'horse'. Both terms are relative to the context—'horse' is relatively specific in the context 'farm', but relatively general in the context 'racing-stable'.

'Abstraction', in turn, is the selection of a given feature common to a number of different entities, or, in Wimsatt's terms, the seeing 'of a number of dissimilar objects under an aspect which they have in common'. Strictly speaking, abstraction is an act, not an entity, the act of classification, not the ensuing product, the general or superordinate class itself. The feature abstracted, since it is a property of an object, is an adjective, for example

[1] Stephen Ullmann, *Language and Style* (Oxford, 1964), p. 117.

[2] *The Prose Style of Samuel Johnson* (New Haven, 1963, paperback edition). See also the interesting discussion of 'subordinate-superordinate' categories in Roger Brown, *Words and Things* (Glencoe, Ill., 1958), Chapter VII.

'equine' or 'horsey'. But we can entitize the property or aspect by a simple grammatical conversion, nominalizing the adjective; thus, it is common usage to extend 'abstraction' to refer to that property or aspect as a thing in itself: 'equinity' or 'horsiness'. The adjectives from which these nouns derive are conceived as representing qualities still *in* the object-nouns they modify: in 'equine animal', 'equine' is not yet an abstract word (in the strict sense) since it has not yet been removed from the object to which it is attributed. Hence, not adjectives, but their nominalizations are the only really 'abstract' words. The same can be said of verbs, since these are also attributed to (predicates of) nouns; thus 'runs' in 'John runs' is not abstract in the sense that 'running' is.

The third contrast is between 'sensory' and 'non-sensory', that is, 'tangible' and 'intangible'. Some things can be experienced through the senses and others not, although this distinction is also relative. Mental actions, no matter how specific, like 'explicate' or 'subtract', are intangible, while very general terms for objects, like 'utensil', are still thought of as tangible.

That is to say, an association between the halves of these three dichotomies—general-abstract-intangible, on the one hand, and specific-concrete-tangible, on the other—is usual but not inevitable.[1] 'Speculate' and 'ponder' are fairly specific as mental acts go, but of course not tangible. Neither are they abstract (in the restricted sense indicated above) since they are not entitized qualities. 'Smoothness', on the other hand, is abstract in the strict sense, and it is tangible, but not specific.

Though sometimes 'abstract' in the narrow sense, the sense appropriate to an author like Samuel Johnson, James' later style is more exactly described as intangible. (Dorothea Krook's phrase 'non-material substance of consciousness' is obviously an attempt to specify this quality. But there are several abstract

---

[1] Although there seem to be some interesting restrictions: 'The more specific the class notion becomes, the more difficult it is to conceive it abstractly or at least to find an abstract word for it . . . "animality" is a more common abstraction than "horsiness" or "equinity", and the latter more common than "colthood" or "coltiness" '—Wimsatt, p. 53.

elements in James besides the psychological.) Further, intangibility (to move, myself, to the abstract noun) is the concomitant
of certain other structural, stylistic and contentual choices.

'Abstract' is often—indeed usually—used more loosely than
this; that is, it often covers all three of Wimsatt's senses. It is not
for me to fight usage; far from criticizing others, I know that the
looser sense of 'abstract' has frequently crept into my own discussion. But which term we use is not so important as is a grasp
of the distinctions. What seems clear is that James does not show
theoretical or philosophical interest in abstractions as such, in
qualities-as-essences, as did Johnson; that his intangibility results
from a preoccupation with mental states and social relations; that
these—as much as, or even more than the characters themselves—
are topics commented upon and hence cast as syntactically important nouns; and finally that other stylistic phenomena, like the
increased metaphorizing of the later novels, might be explained,
in part at least, as a need to prevent intangibility from leading to
dryness.[1]

---

[1] Several of the studies of James' revisions argue that the later style is
more 'concrete', but they are not persuasive. Royal Gettmann, 'Henry James'
Revision of *The American*', *American Literature*, XVI (1945), 279, for example,
speaks of James' search for 'the specific, the concrete, the explicit', and in the
next sentence 'for the exact word'. But the 'exact' word need be neither
'concrete' nor 'explicit'; on the contrary, for the effects that James wanted
they are often intentionally intangible and vague. For Gettmann to say, for
example, that 'I don't care for inanimate canvas or for cold marble beauty'
is a more *concrete* version of 'I don't care for pictures' seems a very peculiar
use of the word.

Sidney J. Krause's study 'James' Revisions of the Style of *The Portrait of a
Lady*', *American Literature*, XXX (1958), pp. 68–73, also argues that James
regularly replaced 'a detached general reference—which might give an idea
more gravity than it needs—with a particular one'; but his examples do not
really show that the changes are such, except in the case of illustrative
physical metaphors.

F. O. Mattiessen's 'The Painter's Sponge and Varnish Bottle', an appendix
to *Henry James: The Major Phase* (New York, 1963), which is another study
of the revision of *The Portrait of a Lady*, also argues that the later James was
more concrete (pp. 175ff.); however, he makes it clear that what he means

2. HOW INTANGIBLE? STATISTICS AND EXAMPLES

I begin, tediously but unavoidably, with figures—to give some idea of *how* intangible the style of James is. Not only are there large numbers of intangible nouns in James' later writing, but these typically fill important syntactic positions, like grammatical subjects. Ian Watt's observation that James has a 'pronounced tendency towards using abstract nouns as subjects of main or subordinate clauses' and that these are very often nouns for mental ideas[1] can be confirmed statistically. In the same sample of James' later style as studied by R. W. Short (the 196 sentences of Chapter Five of *The Ambassadors*), I find that only forty-five per cent of grammatical subjects are nouns referring to human beings. Of the other fifty-five per cent, only six per cent refer to tangible things. Thus, virtually half the subjects in the chapter are intangible. The very first sentence of the novel reveals the trend: it begins not with 'Strether', but with 'Strether's question'. When we look at comparable styles the distribution is quite different; in each of four novels contemporary with *The Ambassadors*, the subject of the first sentence is human: Conrad's *Typhoon* starts with 'Captain Macwhirr,' Butler's *The Way of All Flesh* with 'I', Gissing's *Veranilda* with 'armies', and Forster's *Where Angels Fear to Tread* with a human 'they'.[2]

is the increase in metaphoric imagery (an example is the change from 'their multifarious colloquies' to 'their plunge into the deeps of talk'). But, as I hope to show, one can reasonably take the view that it may very well be a *consequence* of the increase in intangibility that the later style became more metaphoric, as a corrective of dryness.

[1] Watt, p. 470.

[2] George Gissing, *Veranilda* (1905), E. M. Forster, *Where Angels Fear to Tread* (1905), Samuel Butler, *The Way of All Flesh* (1904), and Joseph Conrad, *Typhoon* (1902).

In larger samples (two hundred sentences long), I find that the other four authors have humans performing as subjects at least sixty-seven per cent of the time, while intangible subjects may number as little as fourteen per cent (Conrad) and never more than twenty-two per cent (Butler).

Thus, in James, intangible grammatical subjects outnumber tangible, while in the other styles the reverse is true—and by an average of four to one. The figures for a sample of equal length from *The Wings of the Dove* (Book IV, chapter 1) are only slightly less striking: of 312 subjects, 55 per cent are human and 1 per cent objects, as opposed to 44 per cent intangible nouns. And in *The Golden Bowl* (Book IV, chapter 2), of 275 subjects, 53 per cent are human, 1 per cent objects, and 46 per cent intangible. To the extent that intangible noun-subjects provide an adequate measure, one can say that the style of the later James is at least three times as intangible as that of any of these contemporaries.

It is interesting, further, to compare the later and the earlier Jamesian styles in respect to this feature. In the first version of *The American*, the figures are like those for Gissing, Forster, Butler and Conrad: in a two hundred sentence sample, 71 per cent of subjects are human, 6 per cent tangible things and 23 per cent intangible. But *The Portrait of a Lady* is quite different; in the first two hundred sentences of Chapter Forty-Two, the statistics are very much like those of *The Wings of the Dove*: 56 per cent human subjects, 2 per cent tangible things, and 42 per cent intangible. The 14 per cent decrease in human subjects and the 18 per cent increase in intangible subjects over *The American* is a good indication of the striking change in James' style. Typical of *The American* is 'Newman then started on his travels, with all his usual appearance of slow-strolling leisure, and all his essential directness and intensity of aim'; a sentence in *The Portrait*, on the other hand, is more likely to read 'Her notion of the aristocratic life was simply the union of great knowledge with great liberty; the knowledge would give one a sense of duty, and the liberty a sense of enjoyment.' It is not only the fact that her 'notion', not Isabel, is the subject of the sentence, but also that the predicate is the simple existential copula: not 'Isabel *thought* that . . .' but 'Her notion *was* . . .' The implications of this preference for statements of the existence of abstractions over statements of the actions of characters must be followed, for they seem profound in any consideration of James' style. To say that such preferences are predictable because Isabel is a more reflective person than Newman is not to answer the question, or, at best, it is merely to urge a truism that no one will deny, namely, that style is inevitably a reflection of content.

James' growing preference for abstract over human subjects is plentifully visible in the revisions of the early novels for the 1909 New York edition. Compare the following, from the two versions of *Roderick Hudson* (my italics for grammatical subjects):

1878 Version	*1909 Version*
She was very delicately shaped, and Roderick had come honestly by his physical slimness and elegance.	*Her marked refinement of line and surface* seemed to tell how her son had come by his elegance, his physical finish.
He was attempting in a certain sense to lead the ideal life, and *he* found it at the least not easy.	*The ideal life* had been his general purpose, but the *ideal life* could only go on very real legs and feet . . .
Roderick was peculiarly inscrutable.	*Roderick's reflecting surface* exhibited, for the time, something of a blur.
Here *Rowland* had with his companion a great deal of talk . . .	Here *it* was that *communication for our friends* found its best allies . . .
He could hardly help smiling.	Ah, this pressed the spring, and *his inward irony*, for himself, gave a hum.
Mary's apprehensive face seemed to him an image of his own state of mind.	*Mary's tense smoothness—a serenity with a surface like slippery ice and from which any vain remark rebounded with its heels in the air—* seemed to him an image of his own state of mind.

1878 Version	*1909 Version*
There was a silence; *Rowland* said nothing. . .	There was a silence, *Rowland's share in which* was the intensity of his consciousness of the young woman at the window.

3. LOGICAL TERMS

Consider this sentence from *The Ambassadors*: 'His idea was to begin business immediately.' Or this, from *The Golden Bowl*: 'That impression came back—it had its hours of doing so; and it may interest us on the ground of its having prompted in Maggie a final reflection, a reflection out of the heart of which a light flashed for her like a great flower grown in a night.' What can we say about words like 'idea' and 'impression', about 'business' and reflection', beyond noting their 'abstractness'? Miss Krook has referred to them as 'logical'.[1] But logical in what sense? 'Philosophical'? 'Consequential'? Or merely 'generally intellectual'? Is the witticism that William James' textbooks sound like novels and Henry James' novels like textbooks more to the point? For it doesn't seem that these terms are used in any technically 'philosophical' way. Even so pregnant a word as 'idea' has little speculative interest in such contexts. Or take 'form' or 'essence': Strether stops on the grass, before reaching Maria Gostrey, and goes 'through the form of feeling for something . . . yet the essence of the act was no more than an impulse to gain time.' This is 'form' or 'essence' in nothing like their classical philosophical senses; they could be called 'philosophical' only in deference to associations or connotations that they might bear in other contexts. Their use is far different in the prose of Samuel Johnson, for instance, whose style Wimsatt has shown to be 'philosophical' in a meaningful sense of the word. Rather, in James, they seem

[1] pp. 55-7.

comfortably and unprovocatively accommodated to the social or psychological situation in which they are plumped down. At best they are slightly ironic, in the sense that they are too 'strong', too hyperbolic, for a lightweight world of manners and social situations. James' plots and characters and atmospheres do not seem to justify—except ironically—the intellectual freight that such words bear, and that is perhaps partly the 'intention'.

What sorts of semantic categories do these intangible words fall into? The basic one, obviously, is psychological, arising from the need to depict mental rather than physical activity. His characters are constantly engaged in (or in the grips of) heavy ratiocination: they are forever learning, sensing, reflecting, contemplating, piecing things out, 'looking' at things that 'hover' there before them, and so on. What has been aptly called James' 'cognitive apparatus'[1] is very elaborate indeed. But though the vocabulary is rich, the actual amount of psychological distinction is small, and most of the variety is, like much else in James, elegant variation. The range of mental activity is fairly narrow, in comparison to that of an author like Dostoievsky. Further, James was no more a professional psychologist than a professional philosopher; his psychological terms are not introduced to analyse characters so much as to emphasize that their most characteristic activity is thinking.

4. PSYCHOLOGICAL VERBS

My basic concern is with nouns, but I must first describe the verbs of psychological action, since many nouns are simply derivations of these—for example, 'rationalization' from 'ration-

---

[1] By Michael Shriber, in 'Cognitive Apparatus in *Daisy Miller*, *The Ambassadors* and Two Works by Howells: A Comparative Study of the Epistemology of Henry James', in *Language and Style*, II (1969), pp. 207–25. I owe much to Shriber for the following discussion of psychological verbs.

alize', 'decision' from 'decide' and so forth. Verbs refer to actions rather than to things, so it is somewhat illogical to speak of their tangibility or materiality or the like. But, obviously, overt physical activities, like walking and dancing, may be *perceived* by an outside observer in a direct, physical way, while mental action can only be surmised.

Again it is useful to quote some figures. There are 250 verbs of mental action (tokens, not types) in the two-hundred sentence sample from *The Wings of the Dove*, around 65 per cent of them predicated of Milly.[1] This is almost three times as many as are predicated of Mr. Overton, the narrator of *The Way of All Flesh*, and more than five times as many as of Captain Macwhirr in *Typhoon*. These figures, of course, reflect the content of the novels, and the greater degree to which James maintains a single, limited narrative point of view or 'center of consciousness' since it is precisely by presenting large doses of the inner lives of characters that the limited narrative point of view is established.

Compiling lists of verbs of mental action is a difficult task because there are many marginal cases. It makes best sense to consider only verbs which are *explicitly* mental. Characters are, irrepressibly, thinking beings (at least they were before Hemingway, and the modern 'anti'-novel); and even physical acts cannot be dissociated from mental origins. If we say 'Milly danced', we ordinarily assume that she was conscious of dancing as well as doing it; people are more likely than not to think about what they are doing. But clearly the kinds of mental action we are interested in when we talk about intangibility and abstractness are those which do not have immediate physical concomitants. Any decision will be arbitrary, of course, and there are various kinds of arbitrariness. Verbs which refer to the negation of action may be

---

[1] There are 228 such verbs in the sample from *The Golden Bowl*, of which 175 are predicated of Maggie. For some reason that I cannot explain *The Ambassadors* has smaller totals: Chapter I has 165, with 129 predicated of Strether, and Chapter V has exactly the same overall total. The two versions of *The American* are about equal: the early version has 221 with 169 predicated of Newman and the later 217 with 163 predicated of Newman.

B

indeterminately physical or mental; thus, a verb like 'pause' may or may not have a physical concomitant. If Milly pauses while thinking about X, the pause is a pure mental act; if she pauses while walking down the street, however, the reference is to physical action. A somewhat different problem is how to interpret verbs which are predicated of the *other* characters, the *non*-central-consciousnesses, whose mental life can only be guessed at by the mind in which the reader is placed. For example, when we read at the end of Chapter II of *The Ambassadors* that Waymarsh stared at his washstand like 'Milrose in person', and that he kept on 'considering' the basin and jug as he listened to Strether, we know that 'considering'—though in other applications a verb of mental action—must refer to Waymarsh's behaviour—the fixation of his eyes—as visible to an external observer, Strether. What we have is Strether's interpretation of what Waymarsh is doing, not a direct entrance into Waymarsh's mind. Of course it is ironic: Waymarsh keeps his eyes fixed on the washstand to avoid the embarrassment of crossing glances with Strether; but it is *Strether*'s irony that we share. The verb, however, is 'consider', not 'stared at' or 'fixed his eyes upon' (it is interesting how frequently even external physical acts may be expressed in the language of mental action). Only the context tells us in such cases that the reference is external, not internal.

There are other analytical considerations, too. Not all mental acts are expressed by verbs like 'judge', 'think', and so on. There are many ways—some of them very relevant to a study of intangibility as a stylistic trait—in which the inner life may be evoked without using verbs of explicit mental action. For example, a contrary-to-fact statement like 'It was [to Strether] as if p' amounts to saying 'Strether felt that p, even though p did not literally occur', and so 'be as if' must necessarily be included in our list. There are other kinds of neutral words, too, like time-nouns: 'The hour was filled nevertheless with the effect of his nearness . . .' or 'the moment placed her'. There is, obviously, an ellipsis in both cases of a referential phrase like 'for Maggie', 'for Strether'. Another source is metaphor, which of course occurs bountifully in the later fiction, especially the 'low-grade' sort which does not immediately strike us as such: 'come back' in 'there came back to [Maggie] with it an echo of the long talk they had together, one September day at Fawns . . .'; or 'count for' in 'That occasion might have counted for them . . . as the first step in an existence more intelligently arranged'; or 'fix', in 'She might have been fixing with intensity her projected vision.' A slightly different species is the common synecdoche, like 'Her heart stood still.' There are still other cases that make the determination of an exact list of mental verbs difficult, but my disclaimer is now sufficient; I only trust that my account is extensive enough to represent James' practice adequately.

A rather detailed analysis of the semantics of the verbs of mental action is necessary to underpin any discussion of their counterpart nouns. A recent study of James' cognitive language by Michael Shriber provides an excellent point of departure. If we separate, as is commonly done, a cognitive or judging part of the mind ('John decided that p') from an emotive or feeling part ('John feared X'), we have a rough basis for categorization. (For simplicity's sake we may treat 'volitional' verbs, like 'want' and 'desire' as cognitives.) In each category, we can distinguish between *stages* of ratiocination: (1) perception, (2) cognition (or emotion) proper, and (3) belief (attitude, prejudice). For example, (1) 'John observed Bill's behavior', (2) 'John decided that Bill was an idiot', (3) 'John has always believed that Bill was an idiot'. In (1), a cognition is anticipated but not yet engaged in; that is, no actual predication or assertion is made; in (2) such a predication *is* made—'Bill is an idiot'—and that predication is the result of a genuine cognitive *process*, either accompanied by mental effort, or simply as 'received'; in (3) the process now completed and predication registered, the predication exists in a kind of stasis in the mind; indeed, it need no longer be in the consciousness at all (an attitude or belief is not something which we actively cogitate but one which subsumes our thinking).[1] This, in brief, is Shriber's

[1] Shriber suggests a variety of syntactic consequences of these distinctions: (1) may occur in the progressive aspect whereas (2) and (3) tend not to; (3)

categorization, but it must be elaborated a bit; I introduce a fourth category—namely 'pre-cognition'—half-way between perception and cognition (see below).

(1) 'Perception' can be simply defined as the mental identification and organization of stimuli received by the senses in terms of learned categories. I can 'sense' no more than a trapezoid, with its wider base at the bottom, supported by four narrow perpendicular oblongs: I 'perceive' a table. Now just as we can restrict 'cognition' to the judgment of an assertion (typically marked in indirect discourse by a *that*-clause), we can similarly restrict 'perception' in its literal uses to the recognition or 'placing' of a sensible object: '[Strether] had noticed her the day before, at his previous inn. . . .' The process may include a drawing of intellectual consequences, that is, cognitive overtones: for example, 'Milly perceived that . . . her word about this other person really "drew" him.' On the other hand, 'She might learn from him why she was so different from the handsome girl' is a clear cognition, consisting of the cognizing element 'She might learn from him', and the proposition cognized 'Why she was so different from the handsome girl'. Note that 'learning' is almost by definition a cognizing rather than a perceiving verb: one cannot, for example, learn a sunset or a flower.

What needs to be observed about James' later style is that, unlike that of a novelist such as Robbe-Grillet, it contains relatively few acts of pure perception. When normally perceptual verbs are used, they have strong cognitive implication. What Jamesian characters 'see', for example, is more usually a situation, a moral or psychological issue (generally depicted in a whole clause), than a visible object: 'She seemed even now to see that there might be a good deal they [she and Lord Mark] would get round to', 'She saw how she was justified of her pleas for people and her love of life.' There are ten occurrences of 'see' in my sample from *The Wings of the Dove*, but only two are simple perceptions, and these

but not (1) or (2) may use the simple present tense, in a durative sense; (1) but not (2) and (3) takes manner and result adverbs; only (2) easily takes adverbs of instantaneous time.

(along with one occurrence of 'lose sight of') are the only purely perceptual verbs in the whole passage.

(2) Intermediate between perception and cognition, there is a kind of mental action that can be called 'pre-cognitive'. I introduce this term to name an activity of focusing or dwelling upon something, an object or state of affairs, mental or physical, but without coming to an actual cognition about it; thus, in the series discussed above, intermediate between 'John observed Bill's behavior' and 'John decided that Bill was an idiot' is a statement like 'John pondered Bill's behavior.' Pondering is more than merely observing, but not yet conclusively cognitive. For example, Strether is represented as 'thinking over what [Maria] said'; to 'think over' x is more than merely perceptual, like 'to hear x', but not yet cognitive, like 'to think x'. The example of 'learn' quoted above may be considered again: Milly tells herself that 'She might learn from him why she was so different from the handsome girl—which she didn't know, being merely able to feel it.' Milly's sense of the difference is only pre-cognitive; she had not yet reached a cognitive conclusion, that is, knowledge. Like perception (and unlike cognition, which tends to involve a momentary 'peaking'), this focusing or dwelling-upon activity may continue for a time, in a steady state: indeed one can 'ponder' something indefinitely without reaching a cognition, as he is understood to do when once there occurs a genuinely cognitive verb, like 'decide'. The pre-cognitive condition may be signalled quasi-metaphorically, by a verb whose use is more usually perceptual, for instance 'follow': 'He gazed with unseeing, lingering eyes as he followed some of the implications of his act.' Unlike perception, however, pre-cognition is not directly dependent upon the senses; it may be set off by a perception, or it may not, as when we entertain a thought totally unrelated to the environment, one which just pops into our head. Verbs in this category are used to describe the contemplation of a state of affairs or a proposition, but not an object (the province of perception). It doesn't ordinarily make sense to say 'We pondered the sunset', but we can 'ponder John's situation' or 'ponder John's decision to go'.

Like cognitions, however, pre-cognitions are either active, that is, a positive performance of the mind, or passive, that is, recipient of outside stimulation (terms to be defined more fully below): Strether performs a pre-cognition when it is said that he 'could only listen and wonder and weigh his chance', while he is the recipient of a pre-cognition when it is said that 'he was launched in something of which the sense would be quite disconnected from the sense of the past'.

The pre-cognition is very Jamesian in at least two respects. It reflects the assumption that the thinking of major characters must be nebulous, struggling, even chaotic, at best tentative, at best a dwelling upon notions which might come apart in one's fingers. And this is as it should be; the need to contemplate moral situations—like the need to contemplate beauty—is the real hallmark of sensitive beings. In the passage from *The Wings of the Dove*, as many as a sixth of the psychological verbs are pre-cognitive. The favourite is 'wonder'—obviously a key verb for describing Milly's mental state at the banquet. Some others are 'feel', 'ask herself', 'seek', 'think of', 'go into the idea of', 'give time to (the thought of)', 'make the best of'; among recipient forms are 'thrill', 'encounter', and the copula forms 'be aware that', 'be in a state of', and 'be conscious of'; passive forms are 'be awakened to', 'be beguiled with', 'be taken up by'; forms with Milly as object (included or deleted) are 'suggested' [to her], 'be strange [to her] that', and 'stood out for her that'.

(3) Unlike pre-cognition, cognition proper is a narrowly time-bound activity; it presupposes a state of ignorance or indecision before the cognition and one of knowledge after. At a certain moment in time, then—and it is likely to be thought of as only a moment—the cognitive act occurs. Following Shriber, we can distinguish between the way in which the cognition takes place—whether as an act we perform (hence the verb is 'performant'), something that we achieve through effort, or as an event that happens to us, something that we receive because we are in a fit, receptive condition. When we decide, conclude, infer, guess and so on, we are performing; when we become aware, come to realize,

sense, feel, we are receiving. Different introductory verbs occur with nominalizations: we *make* decisions, conclusions, inferences, guesses, but we *have* awarenesses, realizations, senses, feelings.

It is easier to grasp the distinction between performant pre-cognition and cognition than between recipient pre-cognition and cognition. Since, in the first case we are talking about some-body doing something, it is clear enough whether that doing is conclusive or not. Strether is doing something when he 'wonders' and 'weighs his chance' but those actions reach no conclusion or 'peak'; he is equally doing something when he 'sketches to himself' the impression which Maria has made upon him, but in this case, he has concluded or decided, that is, cognized what that impression is. With recipient verbs, this distinction is sometimes clear too: Strether's being 'launched in something' is more or less inconclusive; in 'The moment placed her [for Strether]', however, something conclusive—a recognition—has taken place, even though it is expressed as happening to Strether rather than as the result of his own effort. But with many recipient verbs it is difficult to determine clearly whether there is a conclusive cog-nition or not. Is 'he turned away to find himself . . . facing a lady' pre-cognitive or cognitive? Is it a dwelling on a state of affairs or is it a learning something in the sense that 'he turned and found himself . . .' would be? When Maria expresses her wish to see Waymarsh again and Strether is reported as 'taking in these things', is it a pondering, or a concluded act of comprehension? The answer seems to be both and neither: such verbs seem to neutralize the distinction in a way which performant verbs ap-parently do not.

Shriber concludes that James' later—unlike his earlier—style, and unlike comparable styles (for example, that of William Dean Howells), strongly prefers recipient to performant or static 'belief' verbs. The central consciousnesses of the late fiction are typically *receivers* of 'felt experience' rather than deciders and judgers. Shriber believes that this reflects a movement away from Puritanism, from a priggish moral decisiveness to a more nat-urely sensitive awareness of the world's complexities. He offers a good example from late in *The Ambassadors*, just before Strether's last interview with Mme De Vionnet. The change from a static reliance on old belief to an increasing openness to insight is principally portrayed by the mental verbs and nouns: 'He reverted in thought to his old tradition, the one he had been brought up on and which even so many years of life had but little worn away; the notion that the state of the wrongdoer, or at least this person's happiness, presented some special difficulty. What struck him now rather was the ease of it—for nothing in truth appeared easier.' Strether first *reverts* to a tradition, a notion—a performant verb of cognition evokes a static belief; but his new self, so much opened by 'European' influences, *is struck* by the ease of Chad's liaison with Mme Vionnet. His receptivity is stylistically confirmed by the use of the recipient verbs 'strike' and 'appear', of which he is made the object.

In many cases, performant verbs are introduced precisely to be negated, thus heightening the impression of an increased reliance on reception: 'Strether couldn't yet measure' how marching with calling-card in hand deviated from Maria's behaviour; on his first sight of Maria 'he would as little have been able to say what had been the sign of her face for him on the first occasion as to name the ground of his present recognition'. These inabilities and negations of performant verbs, like their affirmative recipient counterparts, reflect Strether's initial innocence abroad; they are stylistic affirmations of the content, namely Strether's ignorance, his need for a sentimental education. They have their parallels in Milly's instruction in the complexities of English society and in Maggie's in the hazards of modern marriage.

The vast majority of verbs of mental action—almost three-quarters of those attributable to Milly, for example—are cognitive, and of these the majority are recipient. Literally half are elliptical, that is, make no explicit reference to Milly, leaving it to context and narrative point of view to make clear that she is the ultimate agent. For example, Lord Mark makes a remark which 'suggested something apart'. Or the 'special strong beauty' of English girls 'particularly showed in evening dress'. Naturally enough in an evening of impressions, the favourite verb is 'seem', which occurs no less than eight times. Milly sees the fashionable life of London as a swift current: 'It wasn't, then, as the prospect seemed to show, so difficult to get into the current. . . .' 'Seem', 'appear', and related expressions, like 'be as if', add to the uncertainty, the impressionist haze. Not only does she tend more frequently to receive impressions than to form judgments, but these impressions are usually conjectural and contingent. One struggles constantly with appearances, and one's task is to come to terms with them, to assess them as one may. Of the many verbs in respect to which Milly's consciousness stands as recipient, here are a few: (1) with Milly as explicit or implicit object of a preposition (ellipsis is indicated by parenthesis): 'abide with', 'appear' (to), 'represent' (for), 'hover' (before), 'show her visions of', 'be definite' (to), 'swarm' (for), 'remain with', 'bring home to', 'glimmer' (for), 'be as if' (for), 'present itself' (to), 'reveal herself to', 'be odd' (to), 'be vivid' (to), 'be significant' (to), 'be admonitory' (to); (2) with Milly as direct object: the great Jamesian favourite 'strike' (Kate 'struck her as distinguished and interesting, as in fact surprisingly genial'), as well as 'concern', 'affect', 'draw . . . on', 'move'. That leaves a minority, less than half, with Milly as clear subject, for example: 'She might learn from him why she was so different from the handsome girl.' (Others are: 'have . . . at hand', 'make up her mind that', 'say to herself that', 'generalize' (about), 'see that', 'see how', 'accept', 'make out', 'enrich her idea with', 'reduce . . . to order', 'find', 'choose', 'make the circuit of', 'guess', 'suppose', 'surrender to the inevitability of', 'interpose' (into a conversation with herself), 'understand', 'count with . . . as', 'feel', 'give herself up to', 'turn a (mental) corner', 'think', 'bethink herself that', 'tell', 'recognize', 'mean to', 'perceive', and 'know'.)

The list is extensive and diverse; James' predicates of cognition are as 'elegantly varied' as are the different appellations which he assigns to his characters.[1]

[1] Cf. Watt on elegant variation. Some further recipient verbs from *The Ambassadors* and *The Golden Bowl*: 'colour his adventure with success', 'be prepared to', 'be burdened with', 'be moved to', 'muffle (for him)', 'apply

It is useful also to consider the syntax of recipient forms. In addition to constructions with human actor plus verb of sensing, several others are distinguished by Shriber: (1) the impersonal ('it seemed to A that p'); (2) the passive voice ('A was struck by X' or '. . . by the fact that p'); and (3) the human cognizer as object and the cognition as noun-clause-subject ('That p struck A' or 'The fact that p struck A').[1] I will discuss the impersonal construction later; passive and cognizer-as-object need little discussion since they are merely different surface manifestations of the same kind of deep structure. Note that all three constructions are related, since the human cognizer occurs not as grammatical subject but in oblique function (direct or indirect object, object of a prepositional phrase). We can add a fourth surface-syntactic manifestation of recipient process identical with the passive except that an adjective is used; for example, 'Strether was aware that . . .', 'Strether was conscious that . . .' and the like.

(4) One's 'beliefs' or 'notions' are static in the sense that the cognition has already taken place; and Strether, Milly, and Maggie have their share, if for no other reason than to provide the moral garment that must be rent by the barbs and arrows of Life. I have already cited Shriber's example of how cleverly belief verbs are

to her certainty of', 'convey (for him)', 'express (for him)', 'stand out for him', etc. Additional performant verbs are: 'conceive', 'plea', 'notice', 'catch', 'take in', 'mark', 'analyse', 'fall back on', 'sketch to himself', 'discern', 'appreciate', 'pigeon-hole', 'shrink from', 'suspect', 'follow', 'qualify . . . as', 'arrive at', 'believe', 'measure', 'regret', 'weigh'.

[1] The third in great variety: the object may be the direct object, either alone ('. . . notify Strether', '. . . struck Strether') or as subject of a following predicate ('. . . make him pass his arm'); or as prepositional object (often with the quirky use of prepositions like 'for', 'to', or 'with': 'to determine for Strether . . . an arrest', 'it couldn't have been known to him that . . .'); or as object of a prepositional verb ('that figured to him as . . .'); or as object of an adjective (see below); or perhaps most Jamesian of all, with a deleted object, the object remaining only implicit in the context: after a moment of un-recognition, 'the moment placed her: he had noticed her, the day before, at his inn'; 'that marked his renewal [with Chester] as a thing substantial enough to share'; Maria's remark 'so touched the place that he quite changed color', etc.

introduced precisely to show Stether's Woolett notions giving way under the onslaught of experience. It is Strether's glory, and his salvation (if he really is saved), to rediscover in middle-age the power of learning. But even at the outset he has fewer pre-conceptions than his compatriot Waymarsh; there are comparatively few static verbs in the first chapter, and some of these are negative, thus expressly rejecting the power of belief: 'He had felt during those moments that these elements [of Appearance] were not so much to his hand as he should have liked them', 'He had quite the sense that she knew things he didn't', 'He had believed that he had a limit, but the limit was transcended within thirty-six hours.'

It is worth repeating that some mental action verbs overflow categories or prove difficult to place. This is particularly so in the spaces between perception and pre-cognition and between pre-cognition and cognition: 'What had come as straight to [Strether] as a ball in a well-played game—and caught, moreover, not less neatly—was just the air, in the person of [Maria], of having seen and chosen'. The metaphor is a good representation of the continuum: first the perception, the plain sight of Maria, then the pre-cognitive work, and finally the registration on Strether's understanding. But who is to say when one stops and the next begins? Still, that there are such stages seems important to recognize, particularly if it can be shown, as Shriber has, that James' characters tend to exhibit one kind of mental activity rather than another.

What is clear is that the mental category of many verbs is not determined by the verb itself but by its context. Many verbs which might seem perceptual or pre-cognitive in isolation turn out in context to be cognitive. For example, 'make something out' might strike us as inveterately perceptual, but in James it is often an act of judgment, even when predicated of perceptual organs: Strether's eyes 'make out as much a case for her, in proportion, as her own made out for himself'. Similarly, Strether's 'marking' that Maria's preparation was the model for the occasion of an informal walk is not really a perception, or at least not only a perception.

In short, I think it a mistake to find technically psychological exactness in these verbs. James uses them with no obvious reference to his brother's discipline; they provide a large and various and, above all, interchangeable set of counters for the whole range of mental activity. His exactness is esthetic, not professionally psychological, and it is always open to the freedom of imaginative and metaphorical extension.

5. PSYCHOLOGICAL NOMINALIZATIONS

But my main subject is James' abstractness. The fact that many of James' verbs are psychological does not itself account for the peculiar effect of intangibility that we feel in the later style. After all, novels by other writers include thinking of one kind or another without evoking this effect. It is James' striking tendency to *nominalize* these verbs that greatly increases the intangibility of the style. To transform 'John observed X' or 'John apparently decided that p' into 'John's observation was X' or 'John's decision appeared to be p' is (regardless of the degree of concreteness of 'X' or 'p') to put on stage an abstract entity where previously there had been only a human actor. When you nominalize such a verb, you are presenting an entity for inspection, an entity capable of undergoing full elaboration and qualification, even of becoming (as not infrequently in James) a complete personification.

The transformation of psychological verbs into nouns argues the substantive character of thought. Thoughts and perceptions in James' world are entities more than actions, things more than movements. They occupy a space—the mind; though intangible, they are 'things' *in* the mind. Further, there is established between them and the characters a relation not unlike the relation which characters bear to each other, indeed, one which may be livelier and in some ways more important. Thus it is no accident that abstractions tend to occur in important syntactic positions like that of grammatical subject. Indeed, it often seems as if James created characters as anchors for abstractions rather than abstractions as part of the illusion of character: '. . . the relation between Kate and freedom, between freedom and Kate was a different one from any [Densher] could associate . . . with the girl who had just left him . . .'; 'The new perception bristled for her, as we have said, with odd intimations'; 'The problem bristled the more by reason of poor Strether's fairly open sense of the irony of things.' There is often lively metaphoric ingenuity in the way abstraction is yoked together with character.

The extent to which nominalizations of mental actions are characteristic of the later style can be seen clearly in the 1909 revision of early novels like *Roderick Hudson* and *The American*. In the original of *Roderick Hudson*, for example, Rowland is described simply as having 'always felt a sort of imaginative tenderness for poor little unexplained Giacose'; while in the revised version, we read 'To the personage [Giacosa] so urbanely sounding them his imagination had from the first all benevolently attached itself' (note how the reflexive construction serves further to reify the abstraction). In the original confrontation scene in *The American*, upon hearing Mme Cintré tell Newman to ask *her* why she will not permit the marriage, Mme de Bellegarde is described simply as being 'as pale as her daughter'; in the revision, however, 'her consciousness had paled her face'. Similarly, the marquis 'looked grimly deliberate' becomes 'his deliberation was grim'; and 'You are not proud enough' becomes 'your pride falls short enough'.

The conversion of mental acts into entities through nominalization is an essential device for James; the mind is explored, even to the limits of consciousness, where a character can stand back and watch a parade of mental objects march before him. Consider, for example, Milly's first view of Kate Croy, who makes upon her 'a great impression of beauty and eminence. This impression had remained so with Milly that at present, and although her attention was aware at the same time of everything else, her eyes were mainly engaged with Kate Croy. . . .' Notice how there are three actors in this semantic space, the 'attention', the 'eyes', and the relatively passive Milly herself (we need not inquire too narrowly into the physiology of the case). What is clear and typical is that the impressions and impressed organs grammatically dominate; it is not Milly who 'was aware of' and 'engaged with' the spectacle of Kate, but rather her *attention* which was aware and her *eyes* which were engaged. Milly is only somewhere behind them, watching them operate. This substitution of the organ of perception for the whole person is not an occasional and unmotivated synecdoche but an integral part of James' conception of the self-conscious protagonist; as a consequence, characters leave—and abstractions enter—the grammatical limelight.

The trend is, on occasion, pushed so far that the abstraction literally comes alive, in a personification:

. . . that consciousness, lately born in [Maggie] had been taught the evening before to accept a temporary lapse, but had quickly enough again, with her getting out of her own house and her walking across half the town . . . found breath still in its lungs.

It exhaled this breath in a sigh, faint and unheard . . .

A consciousness which sighs a last unheard breath. Unheard by whom? By the *other* actor, of course, by Maggie, who had been momentarily separated by her seductive husband from this 'companion', this awareness of the need to follow a plan to save her marriage. Later, the two—she and this consciousness-with-lungs—are rejoined, like fellow-conspirators in a secret cell.

Or, a few lines later, an 'impression' becomes a 'witness', even a butler:

Meanwhile . . . the prior, the prime impression had remained, in the manner of a spying servant, on the other side of the barred threshold, a witness availing himself, in time, of the lightest pretext to re-enter. It was as if he had found this pretext in her observed necessity of comparing—comparing the obvious common elements in her husband's and her stepmother's ways of now 'taking' her. With or without her witness, at any rate, she was led by comparison . . .

So confident is the identification that it can figure in a pastparticipal modification with deleted agent: 'Her observed necessity of comparing'—it is the impression-as-spying-servant who observes that she has felt such a necessity. These are the extremes which James permits himself to vivify and dramatize the inner lives of his characters.

Before continuing the discussion of the nominalization of mental verbs I need to say a word about their grammar.[1] It is useful to distinguish between morphological (single-word) and syntactic (word-group) classes.

Morphological nominalizations are of two types: derivational and inflectional. Many nouns are derived from verbs or adjectives by the addition of suffixes: *impress* plus *-ion* gives *impression*, *enjoy* plus *-ment* gives *enjoyment*, *tight* plus *-ness* gives *tightness*, *active* plus *-ty* gibes *activity*, etc. In some cases, the suffix is zero: *to drive* plus zero suffix gives *a drive*. Derived nouns are fully nouns. They have non-terminal suffixes, that is, they permit further suffixation, derivational and inflectional: *impressions*, *impressionism*, *impressionisms*; *enjoyments*; *tightnesses*; *activities*. Further, they may occur with every form of nominal modifier: *the impressions*, *any of these impressionisms*, and so on. In some cases their derivation is concealed by history, their etymological sources not currently existing as separate words in English. The objects of the verb from which the nominalization derives (if preserved) are regularly expressed as *that*-clauses or as objects of a preposition, usually but not necessarily *of*: 'the understanding that they should meet at Chester', 'his enjoyment of it' [i.e. Waymarsh's presence]. The agent, the underlying grammatical subject, if preserved, is a genitive or the object of a preposition: 'Strether's question', 'the decision *for* Strether . . .' and the like. But the agent is also frequently the grammatical object; thus 'Strether's impression of her' derives from 'She impressed Strether', and 'that Strether could wait without disappointment' is related to 'Waymarsh's absence did not disappoint him'.

[1] For a recent treatment see Chapter III of Robert Lees, *The Grammar of English Nominalizations* (Bloomington, 1960). See his footnote 41 (p. 108) for the distinction between derived and inflectional nominalizations.

In inflectional nominalization, on the other hand, the suffixation is done not by history, as a permanent part of the word, but for the nonce, by the speaker. Endings are final; nothing can follow them. The only inflectional form to concern us here is the gerund, made in English by adding *-ing* to the base of the verb. We can distinguish two kinds: 'action gerunds' and 'fact gerunds'.[1] A recent study provides a nice set of contrasts:

Action gerund: 'His drawing of the sketch fascinated me because he always did it lefthanded.'
Fact gerund: 'His drawing the sketch fascinated me because I didn't know he could be persuaded so easily.'
Derived noun: 'His drawing fascinated me because it was so large.'

The action gerund focuses on the manner of the act, something like 'The way he drew the sketch was what fascinated me', whereas the fact gerund focuses on the fact that he performed such an act: 'That he drew . . .' or 'The fact that he drew the sketch was what fascinated me.' In the third example, *drawing* is no longer a gerund but an ordinary noun, like *sketch* or *picture*; it takes a plural, we can speak of 'a drawing', 'drawings', etc. Several features distinguish action and fact gerunds, but the chief is illustrated in the example, namely that action gerunds require *of* before their objects and fact gerunds do not.[2]

It should be clear from these examples that gerunds and other *-ing* nouns fall prey to ambiguity rather easily. Not only the difference between action and fact gerund, but that between gerund and derivative noun can easily be lost in the absence of sufficient context. For example, 'His drawing fascinated me' in isolation could have any of the three senses. And because of the

---

[1] My terms correspond to Lees' 'action nominals' (ibid., pp. 64–9) and 'gerundive nominals' (pp. 71–3).

[2] Others, according to Lees: 1. active gerunds do not preserve auxiliaries but fact gerunds may (not 'His having drawn of the picture'); 2. active (but not fact) gerunds may change adverbial modifiers to adjectives ('His rapid drawing of the picture'); 3. active gerunds may not occur for some verbs, but fact gerunds always do (not 'His having of a hat', but 'His having a hat').

heavy use that James makes of gerunds,[1] ambiguities of this sort do sometimes arise: 'Nothing could have been more odd than Strether's feeling, at that moment, that he was launched in something of which the sense would be quite disconnected from the sense of his past' could mean either 'Nothing was odder than the way Strether felt that he was launched . . .' (and so on) or 'Nothing was odder than the fact that Strether felt that way', or 'Nothing could be odder than a certain feeling that Strether had, namely . . .' Gerunds are gratuitously introduced into the revisions of the early novels, like *Roderick Hudson*, as if to increase the complexity of statement: the original 'He [Rowland] tried to have some especial talk with her [Mary], but her extreme reserve forced him to content himself with such response to his rather urgent overtures as might be extracted from a keenly attentive smile' is changed in its last phrase to read '. . . as might be extracted from her leaving him, very frankly, all the consciousness of them' ('them' must refer back to 'overtures': for difficult pronoun reference in James' later style, see below). This could mean either '. . . from the fact that she left him X' or 'from the way in which she left him X'.

So much for the grammatical form of the nominalized verbs. As one would expect, their semantic variety in the Jamesian style is equally complex. They may be analysed in terms of the categories discussed above: perception, pre-cognition, cognition, and belief, but their semantics is more complicated than that of the verbs from which they derive. Regardless of category, verbs (including gerunds) refer only to the act or experience named, not to its object or subject. But a noun derived from a verb might refer to any of the three—subject, action, or object—or to a combination of them. This trichotomy cuts across the distinctions we have already recognized, presenting a rather complex set of categories.

A noun or nominalization may refer to the *act* of perception, cognition, or whatever; or to the mental *faculty*, the part of the

[1] About 16 per cent of the nominalizations in Chapter I of *The Ambassadors* are gerunds.

mind performing it; or to the *object* focused upon. Thus: 'John's perception of the disaster was sudden' refers to the act; 'John's perception is always sudden' refers to the mental faculty; and 'We decided that John's perception of the disaster was incorrect' refers to the thing-perceived. (English sometimes marks the distinction with different forms: thus *knowing* refers to the act, *knowledge* to the thing, and *knowledgeability* to the faculty.) These distinctions tend to be easily blurred, and in many contexts it is impossible to tell precisely which is operative. Out of context, 'John's perception was sudden' could be any one of the three. The context must be inspected carefully and the possibility of ambiguity recognized. There are certain identificational marks worth noting, however, namely that (everything else being equal) an indefinite article or possessive pronoun, especially combined with durative or iterative adverbs, suggests the faculty, while a relative clause or a phrase modifying the noun of perception suggests the thing-perceived. The plural ('perceptions') eliminates reference to the faculty. Further, nominalizations which do not take *that*-clauses or *of*-phrases cannot refer, say, to thing-divined because one can say 'the divination that *p*'. Thus 'taste' can refer to the thing-tasted because one can say 'the taste of *N*', but 'attention' cannot refer to 'thing-attended' because one cannot say 'the attention that *p*' or 'the attention of *N*' (where *N* is object).

The fluidity of meaning and use of the nominalization can be illustrated by one of James' favourites, 'sense'. James' growing fondness for the word may be adduced from its frequent introduction into the revisions; for example, in *Roderick Hudson* the original 'In conversation he was a colourist' is changed in the New York edition to 'His plastic sense took in conversation altogether the turn of colour.' The sense of 'sense' is various and often ambiguous: consider '. . . When [Strether] gazed into the irremediable void of [the palace's] site the historic sense in him might have been freely at play'. The reference here is clearly to a faculty or part of the mind at work; the focus is clear because of the continuity of the predicate, 'been at play'. But shortly thereafter: 'It took as it had not been done yet the form of a question—

the question of what he was doing with such an extraordinary sense of escape. This sense was sharpest after he read his letters . . .' Here what is referred to is the thing-sensed, 'sense of escape' being equivalent to 'sense that he has escaped'; the intangible is handled as if it were tangible, held at arm's length and examined with characteristic incredulity ('What was he *doing* with it?').[1] Less clear is the first sentence of Book Four of *The Wings of the Dove*: 'It had all gone so fast after this that Milly uttered but the truth nearest to hand in saying to the gentleman on her right . . . that she scarce even then knew where she was: the words marking her first full sense of a situation really romantic.' The *of*-phrase following 'sense' seems to commit us to a thing-sensed interpretation, yet the lack of time-specification makes it impossible to eliminate completely the possibility of reference to an act—'her first full sensing of . . .' Is there a hint that this was perhaps the first time that she was capable of knowing what the 'really romantic was', that the power to make such a discernment was only just developing in her?

The categorization of nominalizations best follows the same order as of the mental verbs upon which they are based, that is, perception, pre-cognition, cognition and belief.

(1) As for perception, the word itself is often used, for example, 'Milly could not . . . have said whether, with her quickened perceptions, she were more enlivened or oppressed.' All of the senses are represented, but particularly that of sight. 'Vision' is an extremely popular word in James. The word often means little more than physically 'seeing', or 'thing seen', an instance of his penchant for hyperbole. For example, Maggie observes that despite Amerigo's absence, 'the hour was filled nevertheless with the effect of his nearness, and above all with the effect, strange in an intimacy so established, of an almost renewed vision of the facts of his aspect.' When Strether sees Maria Gostrey for the second time, and her features are described as coming 'back to him as from a recent vision', not much more is meant than that

---

[1] What I would call (somewhat heavy-handedly, I fear) a 'low-grade concretizing metaphor'.

he had seen her before. Similarly, when he sees Mme Vionnet in Notre Dame, 'The moments had already, for that matter, drawn their deepest tinge from the special interest excited in him by his vision of his companion's identity with the person whose attitude before the glimmering altar had so impressed him.' ('Vision of identity with' is a peculiar collocation, and it is not entirely clear whether perception or cognition is involved here: 'vision' can mean either 'view' or 'realization'.) More commonplace is reference to the organ: 'The smallest things, the faces, the hands . . . were all touches in a picture and denouements in a play, and they marked for her, moreover, her alertness of vision.' Another sentence combines olfactory and auditory images, showing how diverse the perceptual appeal can be: 'the very air of the place, the pitch of the occasion had for her so positive a taste and so deep an undertone.' It is worth observing that the senses other than sight and hearing are almost inevitably metaphorical; it is hard to think of an occasion in a novel of James when a real taste is tasted or a real smell smelled.[1]

There are many other nouns representing perception, since naïve heroes are constantly engaged in that process. For example, *seeing* and *taking*: '. . . the kind of mind that thus, in [Milly] made all for mere seeing and taking is precisely one of the charms of our subject'; *notice*: 'Lord Mark . . . attracted their hostess' notice'; or *view*: 'All [Milly] had meant to do was to insist that [Kate's] face was fine; but what she had in fact done was to renew again her effect of showing herself to its possessor as conjoined with Lord Mark for some interested view of it.' Note the characteristic ambiguity: is the view nothing more than the act of looking at Kate or is it rather her face as perceived, some already achieved mental registration about her appearance? Or both? Compare James' way with similar words like 'impression', 'divination', and so on.

James' vocabulary is particularly rich in words for 'thing-

---

[1] See Robert Gale, *The Caught Image* (Chapel Hill, 1964), pp. 175–9, for additional examples. Surprisingly, next to visual images, Gale finds taste images most frequent and auditory images least so.

perceived', where the reference is to some abstracted property of the object of perception. One can find single pages filled with such words: 'prospect', 'indications', 'sign', 'appearances', 'image', 'view', and so forth. The human perceiver is regularly object rather than subject: 'indications', for example, means that something has been indicated *to* Strether. The extensiveness of this class of words clearly indicates that James is less concerned with the things of the world than with the view of those things that characters have and the meanings that are thus registered in their minds.

(2) 'Pre-cognition' has been introduced to represent a kind of mental action in which an object or state of affairs is contemplated, either after a perception, or with no initiating perception, and which itself suggests no cognitive conclusion (although one may follow). The category is equally applicable to nominalizations. To say that Strether had a 'consciousness of freedom' is not to say that he 'perceived' his freedom in any strict sense of the word 'perceived', since 'freedom' is not a perceptible object; neither is 'consciousness' a cognition in the sense that it implies a decision or conclusion. Of course, pre-cognitions may *lead* to cognitions. A clear example occurs in *The Golden Bowl*: Maggie observes a 'process' in her husband of 'weighing something in the balance, of considering [pre-cognitive], deciding, dismissing [cognitive]' (note how the ellipsis of the object strengthens the impression of contemplating, of 'dwelling upon'). Further, the performant/recipient distinction can be observed in pre-cognitive nominalizations as well as verbs. Strether's 'sharper survey of the elements of Appearance than he had for a long time been moved to make' is clearly performant and also clearly pre-cognitive, since there is no consummation: 'a survey' is a kind of pondering or contemplating and could continue indefinitely. Strether's 'sense of his past', on the other hand, is recipient.

Many recipient nominalizations, like their verbal counterparts, presume no distinction between cognition and pre-cognition. Strether's 'taste of change' upon arriving in Liverpool is indeterminately a discovery of a feeling and a contemplation. Similarly, in the statement that there were mixed with his present views of the English countryside 'certain images of his inward picture'— 'images' refers indiscriminately to having these memories and to the fact that they occurred at that particular moment.

(3) As for genuine cognitions, the pages of the late novels display a rich abundance of every category I have mentioned. Among grammatical subjects alone, the following can be found in my short samples: among 'organ' or 'part-of-the-mind' nominalizations: 'fancy', 'imagination', 'sense'; among 'act-of-cognizing' nominalizations: 'imaginations', 'recognition', 'discrimination', 'deciding', 'reasoning', 'admonition', 'renouncement', 'engagement', 'reaction', 'intention', 'deciding', and 'dismissing'; and among 'thing-cognized' nominalizations: 'scheme', 'plan', 'delusions', 'solution', 'discriminations', 'recollection', 'recognition', 'conception', 'vision', 'image', and 'assumption'. Note how many of these are derivations of verbs of saying, mental acts in which the character addresses himself, that is, is both subject and object: 'More than once . . . [Strether] regarded himself as admonished, but the admonition, this morning, was formidably sharp'; 'Was he to renounce all amusement for the sweet sake of that authority? And *would* such renouncement give him for Chad a moral glamour?' (The continuum can as easily go the other way; dialogue or remembered dialogue may be couched in the language of cognition: 'She remembered Fanny Assingham's old judgment, that friend's description of her father and herself as not living at all.')

Cognitions have been defined as mental acts in which something is consummated, some conclusion is reached within the limits of the sentence. Its clearest representative is 'decide': 'John decided to go.' Beliefs, on the other hand, are positions held on the basis of earlier cognitions or emotions. Exactly how much time must elapse before a cognition or emotion has occurred and has been transformed into belief is sometimes unclear. When Strether, 'surveying the elements of Appearance', is disturbed by the feeling 'that these elements were not so much to his hand as he should have liked', and falls back 'on the thought that they were precisely a matter as to which help was supposed to come from that he was about to do', the moment when that thought entered his mind is left vague, but clearly it is recent, since one cannot imagine him having had it in Woolett. Indeed, the thought must have occurred to him only some seconds before; yet it is a *fait accompli* and, as such, a belief held, rather than a cognition made.

(4) Belief nominalizations, unlike pre-cognitions and cognitions, refer only to the 'thing-believed'. Perhaps because of the unsettled state of Strather's mind, and as a token of his open-mindedness, there are very few beliefs recorded in the first chapter of *The Ambassadors*. On the other hand, James seems occasionally to represent as belief what would seem more directly expressible as cognition: when Strether modestly protests that Maria Gostrey could not have heard his name before, 'he had his reasons for not being sure that she perhaps might'. From what he had already seen of her, he believed that she was literate enough to catch the allusion to Balzac. The preference for a belief-form like 'reasons' for a cognitive notion like 'decide' suggests a momentary withdrawal of the microscopic focus on Strether's mind, the kind of withdrawal noted by Lubbock, and which turns up in other stylistic features as well, for example, the occasional direct self-reference to the author-narrator as 'I'. It is possible to refer to such beliefs or reasons without telling us what they are, to leave that to inference, but the expression of a positive act of cognition necessarily makes explicit all there is to know about what happened in the forefront of the character's mind. James was perfectly prepared to withdraw the point of view from his central consciousness when he had some other effect in mind; as Wayne Booth has pointed out so well,[1] he was more interested in an overall *intensity* of effect than in slavish adherence to any single technique.

I have not yet discussed the category of emotion, except as an opposite pole to cognition. Like cognition it may or may not have an external stimulus conveyed through a perception, and it may or may not lead to a belief (or more properly, a prejudice). Like cognitions, emotions can be distinguished—at least syntactically—as either performant or recipient, although in some

[1] In *The Rhetoric of Fiction* (Chicago, 1961), p. 59.

deep semantic sense, all emotion is essentially recipient, as the old term, 'passion', since specialized, clearly suggests. Thus, nominalizations occur in which the 'emoter' is either subject or object of the underlying verb. Examples of the first in the samples are 'enjoyment', 'fear', 'doubt' (if that is really an emotion and not a stimulus to an emotion), 'ache' (not physical), 'vibration', 'desire', 'quickening'; of the second, 'delight', 'exhilaration', 'surprise', 'disgust', 'fatigue', and 'amusement'.

But there is not much pure expression of emotion in James. Many forms are pseudo-emotive, often hyperbolical; the central consciousness is forever 'fearing', 'delighting in', 'enjoying', 'doubting', 'feeling exalted by' matters of relatively little moment. Or at least it's not clear that he is not playing at emotion. An example is Strether's mock-flirtatious language in Chapter I: 'Oh, I'm afraid of you', he says to Maria, afraid of 'falling thus, in twenty minutes, so utterly into your hands . . . nothing more extraordinary has ever happened to me.' 'Falling into your hands' is strong language for what in fact is happening. A moment later he begs her to get him out, out of the 'terror' of 'always considering something else, something else, I mean, than the thing of the moment. The obsession of the other thing is the terror. I'm considering at present, for instance, something else than *you*.' The 'obsession', of course, is little more than a puritanic inability to enjoy the present, the sin of ignoring the here and now, the absorption in what Dr. Johnson calls 'looking into futurity'. That it's a 'terror' for Strether may be a mark of his excruciating sensitivity, but it is also a kind of delicate social manoeuvre. He confesses the truth and yet in so exaggerated a way as to make it socially comfortable. His flirtation with Maria can never become serious but must remain in part a way of being polite. We seem to be touching something very characteristic in the failure of Strether's emotions to bear fruit or even to be what they claim. But then of course Maria is only 'the most unmitigated and abandoned of *ficelles*!'

6. OBLIQUITY

I have argued that by nominalizing verbs of mental action, James makes *them*, rather than the mere human to whom they attach, the topic of the discourse. Grammatically, this entails the partial or total elimination of the real actor, his removal to an oblique position or even complete disappearance. The change may be in one of several directions: from the subject to a pre-positional genitive modifier ('Strether's decision'), to subject or object of a modifying clause ('hadn't it been on the ground that he was tired . . .'), to a direct object ('The fact struck him'), to the object of a prepositional phrase, to modifier of a complementary structure ('This restlessness became his temporary law', 'It was the soreness of his remorse that . . .') and in a variety of other ways. Even in the first paragraph of *The Ambassadors*, as Mr. Watt has so ably shown, this grammatical submergence of character sets the tone: 'Strether's first question . . . was about his friend' (instead of 'Strether first asked about his friend'); 'The same secret principle . . . that had prompted Strether . . .' (instead of 'Strether was prompted by a secret principle', or ' . . . acted under a secret principle'); 'the principle . . . had been with the most newly disembarked of the two men wholly instinctive' (instead of 'Strether instinctively relied on the principle . . .'); and so on.

In obliquing by preposition, James often introduces a stylistic highlighting—or 'foregrounding', as the Czech formalists call it—by an unusual lexical choice. Note how *for* is used in the following sentence: '. . . his business would be a trifle bungled should he simply arrange that this countenance [Waymarsh's] should present itself to the nearing steamer as the first "note", for him, or Europe' (instead of 'should he encounter this countenance as the first "note" of Europe' or the like).[1] Or *in*: 'these things

---

[1] One of my favourites, from *The Wings of the Dove*, is: 'This apprehension, however, we hasten to add, enjoyed for him, in the immediate event, a

were early signs in him that. . .'. Or *on*: 'the apprehension on Strether's part, that . . .; or *with*, in the sense of French *chez*: 'the principle . . . with the most newly disembarked of the two men'; and so on. The oblique situation of the characters, of course, results from making them recipients rather than actors, but James seems to go out of his way to point up the *oddness* of that situation. Why? Perhaps, because, as the Czech formalists argue, foregrounding leads to disautomatization, the breaking-up of habitual and hence stereotyped linguistic responses. When James says 'the principle had been with the most newly disembarked of the two men wholly instinctive', not only does he build a mere wish, at best half-conscious, into a veritable intellectual edifice, a 'principle', but he places it in a very special relation to the person acting under it. To say 'with' Strether is to suggest among other things that Strether is more domain than performer, that the principle pervades, floods Strether's thinking; the effect is quite different from saying 'Strether's principle', which implies that Strether had some control over it, that it was at least *his* principle.

I note that in several of these sentences James' preference is for neutral rather than personal determiners—'the', 'a', 'this', rather than 'Strether's' or 'his', 'a sharp sense' not 'his sharp sense', 'this happier device' not 'the happier device which he hit upon', or the like. Not the least important consequence is that the reader's very effort to supply the personal reference of these notes, principles, devices, consciousness and so on commits him more resolutely to the role of inspector of Strether's mind.

The furthest reach of obliquity, of course, is the complete disappearance of the human agent, and this is a frequent occurrence in the later style, one of the several kinds of ellipsis that James grew to fancy. Of course there is a reference somewhere, if we look hard enough: the reader's ingenuity, or at least his memory, is continually taxed. 'What carried him [Strether] hither and yon was an admirable theory that nothing he could do would not be in some manner related to what he fundamentally had on

certain merciful shrinkage' (instead of 'this apprehension lasted only a minute' or the like).

hand, or *would* be—should he happen to have a scruple—wasted
for it. He did happen to have a scruple—a scruple about taking no
definite step till he should get a letter; but this reasoning carried
it off.' A typical late Jamesian turn; an admirable but not explicitly
identified theory carries Strether hither and thither, an abstraction
made even more dominant by the *what*-construction, at the expense of the mere human it buffets about.[1] The subject of the
that-clause defining 'theory' is no less vague: 'nothing he could
do', which in turn is related to 'what he fundamentally had on
hand', a slangish, breezy summary of his whole delicate project
(see the discussion of colloquial elements below). Then the
outlandish italics of 'would', which might be taken for a confused instant as a correction of the previous 'would not', in a not
unJamesian paradox, but which turns out simply to be the
auxiliary for 'wasted'. Then the whole sentence is negated:
Strether does in fact have a scruple. And that brings us to a
thudding climax, that is, if we manage to grasp that 'this reasoning' (note, not '*Strether*'s reasoning') is in fact the theory, and the
'it' which is 'carried off' (a racy two-word verb) is the scruple.

Or consider this: '. . . having, as he had often privately expressed
it, Paris to reckon with, he threw these hours of freshness consciously into the reckoning. They made it continually greater,
but that was what it had best be if it was to be anything at all. . . '
'It' is 'Paris', 'that' is 'greater', and 'They' are 'the hours of freshness', which only the context tells us are *his* hours of freshness.
The unadorned demonstrative gives these hours an independence
which is later supported by referring to them as 'they' (indeterminately the plural of human and neuter pronouns); it was not
that he had these hours and used them to his own purpose, but
that 'they' descended upon him.

Another example. Strether feels guilty about enjoying himself
too much: 'More than once, during the time, he had regarded
himself as admonished; but the admonition, this morning, was
formidably sharp'. The man is admonishing himself, but the
admonition takes on a life of its own, perhaps depicting some

---

[1] See the discussion of 'cleft constructions' below.

conflict between (the terms are irresistible) superego and id. 'The' in its somber neutrality upholds the faith, Woolett and all that, while the personal pronoun is reserved for that poor admonishable part of Strether that can't help enjoying itself.

It is perhaps the emotive expressions that sound the oddest when freed of personal reference and given a life of their own: Strether's sense of change 'promised already, if headlong hope were not too foolish, to color his adventure with cool success'; Maggie hits upon the idea of 'sharing with [*Amerigo*] whatever the enjoyment, the interest, the experience might be'; Milly decides that Lord Mark's intentions don't matter, so 'suspicion . . . with this, simplified itself . . .' (note the reflexive pronoun, a way of emphasizing the self-sufficiency of the abstraction).

Or the deleted real actor may be the implied subject of some peculiar past participial modifier: on only two pages of *The Golden Bowl* there are references to 'recovered identities', 'questions unanswered', 'dismissed vision', 'observed necessity', 'mitigated midnight', 'worked-out scheme', 'placed chair', and 'barred threshold'. This structure, of course, is a transform of a relative clause: 'identities which they recovered', 'scheme which she worked out', and so on. The habit is so confirmed that even where James feels he must name the original subject, he does so obliquely: 'it all came back in consequence to some required process of their own . . .' (rather than ' . . . to some process which they required' or the like). The developed partiality for the past participial modifier is clearly evident in the frequency with which it is introduced into the revised novels. In *Roderick Hudson*, 'He had caught instinctively the key-note of the Old World' becomes 'He had caught instinctively the key-note of the general, the contrasted European order'; 'It was a very good thing certainly that idleness should prove an experiment to sit heavily on his [Roderick's] conscience' becomes 'It was a very good thing that tried debauchery should so particularly *not* lead him on' (note too the second ellipsis—'on to what?'); 'Rowland in the geniality of a mood attuned to the mellow charm of a Roman villa . . .' becomes 'Rowland, in the geniality of a mood attuned to all the stored patiences that lurk in Roman survivals'; ' "I was seized with a kind of exasperation, a reaction against all this mere passive enjoyment of grandeur" ' has added to it ' ". . . and, above all, against this perpetual platitude of spirit under imposed admirations" '; 'Rowland took immense satisfaction in his companion's lively desire to transmute all his impressions into production' becomes '. . . satisfaction in . . . the instinct of investing every gain of sense or soul in the enterprise of planned production'; 'He saw that the lady's irritated nerves demanded comfort from flattering reminiscence' becomes ' . . . he saw that the poor woman's irritated nerves required the comfort of some accepted overflow. . . .' The increase in complex abstraction is considerable.

By this device, an action which is normally thought of as *affecting* an object becomes transformed into its *property* and the human actor disappears completely in the reduced syntax. By repositioning it, this transformation adds enormously to its importance, at the expense of the submerged human agent. Strether picks up his letters and '. . . after a controlled impulse to go into them in the reception-room of the bank . . . he slipped them into the pocket of his loose gray overcoat . . .' That impulse is Strether's, of course, but in a way it seems quite separated from him: it floats alone there in the reception room, as if its agent had departed the scene or perhaps never even arrived. The next sentence exhibits the same feature: 'Waymarsh, who had had letters yesterday, had had them again today, and Waymarsh suggested, in this particular, no controlled impulses'. This means nothing so simple as 'Waymarsh told Strether to control his impulses'; rather 'Waymarsh' is a kind of synecdoche for 'Waymarsh's behavior' or 'what Waymarsh did', the mere surface representation of a construction of which an abstract noun, since deleted, was really the subject (thus itself an abstraction). Logically, 'Waymarsh' is object, not subject; the construction ultimately goes back to something like 'Waymarsh acted in a way that suggested that he did not control his impulses'; but we are at two removes from that by the intangible grammar.

The effect of this intentional avoidance of the genitive or other means of personal reference is like that of the heavy and indiscriminate use of pronouns, for example, a single 'he' where two men are interacting. The reader is supposed to figure things out on his own. It is a kind of prose that insists upon selecting its own audience, an audience, as Vernon Lee puts it, which is 'accustomed to bear things in mind'.

7. OTHER SOURCES OF NOMINALIZATIONS

I have discussed only nominalizations of psychological verbs, but nominalizations of psychological adjectives are also a rich source of intangible terms for James. Predicate adjectival constructions, of course, are very frequent: Strether 'had been indifferently aware of the number of persons who esteemed themselves fortunate in being, unlike himself, "met" ' ('aware' is a great favourite); 'he was prepared to be vague to Waymarsh about the hour of the ship's touching'; and so on. But it is as easy for adjectives as for verbs to be converted into abstract nouns: for 'aware' to become 'awareness', for 'vague' to become 'vagueness', and so on. We can watch the process at work in the revision of the early novels; the original Mrs. Hudson 'was a small eager woman, with a pale troubled face which added to her apparent age' becomes 'She was a small, softly-desperate woman, whose desperation gave her a false air of eagerness'. Strether's 'double consciousness' showed 'detachment in his zeal and curiosity in his indifference'; Milly 'thrilled, she consciously flushed, and turned pale with the certitude—it had never been so present—that she should find herself completely involved'; Maggie finds herself 'in the act of plucking [a plan] out of the heart of her earnestness'.[1]

---

[1] But adjectives are a much less rich source than verbs; of forty-nine psychological nominalizations in *The Wings of the Dove*, only five (ten per cent) are derived from adjectives.

There are many psychological nouns, of course, that are not nominalizations, and James uses these as handily. They tend to refer to the organ or part of mind ('attitude', 'conscience', 'state of mind', 'spirit', 'wit', and so on) or to the thing conceived ('idea', 'theory', problem', 'category', 'example'), rather than to the act. Acts are likely to derive from verbs, although some, like 'reverie', have no verbal counterpart (in English, at least).

What has been said about the register of verbs of mental action is equally true of the nouns: they do not represent a desire for narrowly exact and professional nomenclature, but rather an attempt to catch the mind at work, in all its uncertainty, indeed, assuming uncertainty to be its ordinary lot, experience to be essentially fluid, and so the narrative task necessarily approximative. This attitude is reflected in other features as well, for example, in authorial intercession in which the narrator confesses momentary ignorance of the contents of the central consciousness. (And not only where such ignorance seems justifiable, for example in the admittedly difficult case of representing the consciousness of a child, like Maisie 'I may not even answer for it that Maisie was not aware of how . . . Mrs. Beale failed to share [Sir Claude's] all but insurmountable distaste for their allowing their little charge to breathe the air of their gross regularity . . .' but also in adult centres of consciousness as well: for example, in response to Maria's observation that Strether might not be enjoying their walk as much as he ought, '. . . he appeared thoughtfully to agree.'[1])

So it would be misguided to insist too strenuously on psychological as opposed to esthetic accuracy or precision in these terms.

[1] On the other hand, there was a great and increasing concern to insure that the descriptions of inner mental states were by the character himself, as part of the illusion of central consciousness, rather than by some intrusive narrator. There are many revisions in *The American* of the following sort: 'he had an exquisite sense of beauty' becomes in the revised edition 'he had what he called an intimate sense of beauty'; and 'conscientiously and impartially' becomes 'and, as he would have said, with detachment'. 'As he would have said' is a typical Jamesian interpolation of the sort we might call 'authority tag'. Booth discusses James' occasional authorial intercession in a sensible way, pp. 44–5.

For one thing, they are endowed with many and often divergent meanings. I have already discussed the distinction between organ, act and thing, but let me mention another example. 'Sense' may be a synonym of 'fancy' or 'imaginative faculty' ('[Strether's] historic sense . . . might have been freely at play'), but it may also refer to the perceiving organs, or to a faculty of the mind 'analogous to sensation' (e.g. 'The moral sense'), or to a 'special capacity for perception, estimation, appreciation, etc.' ('sense of humor'), or to 'clear or sound mental faculties', or to 'any more or less vague perception or impression' ('a sense of security'), or to a 'mental discernment, realization or recognition' of something ('a just sense of it'), or to 'the recognition of something incumbent or fitting' ('a sense of duty'), or to 'sound practical intelligence' ('he has no sense'), or to 'an opinion or judgment formed or held' ('the sense of the meeting').[1] I do not doubt that each of these occurs somewhere in James' work, for he makes the fullest use of the whole resource of the lexicon and also of the plurisignification of individual words. Further, it is precisely this sort of word whose significance becomes a kind of synecdoche for the whole of the mental process. The blurring of the nuance of expression of the mental state may well be 'intentional', an attempt to secure a greater heightening of the fact of consciousness itself.

Indeed, mental action is so important in James that its mere presence is often all that need be cited. One of James' characteristic habits is to tell us no more than that a character *had* a thought about something, that he was 'affected', 'impressed', 'conscious', or whatever, without telling or even implying 'by' or 'of' what. For example, '[Strether] had his association with [Mrs. Newsome's] ruche, but it was rather imperfectly romantic': the point is not what the association was but rather the inevitability that Strether should *have* one. Having associations, being in relations, making speculations—those are the important things: their contents are almost trivial, almost not our business. Charlotte 'stalks' Maggie: 'So definite a quest for her, with the bridge-party interrupted or altered for it, was an impression that fairly assailed the

[1] From *The American College Dictionary*.

Princess . . .' It is the onslaught of the impression—not what that impression is—that is crucial. Milly realizes that 'she had never . . . been in such a state of vibration; her sensibility was almost too sharp for her comfort'; Strether awaits his reunion with Waymarsh 'with something that he would have been sorry, have been almost ashamed not to recognize as emotion, yet with a tacit assumption, at the same time, that emotion would in the event find itself relieved.' The effect is more than amply evident in the revisions. In the original version of *Roderick Hudson*, we read 'The girl beside him pleased him immensely'; in the revision, she 'appealed, strangely, to his sense of character'. But 'appealed' how? Clearly the psychology is subtler, more tentative and allusive. Similarly, '. . . Roderick should not . . . have been captivated . . .' becomes 'Roderick should not . . . have received his impression.' We can only infer that the 'impression' is one of captivation or the like. And instead of 'an instinctive vision of how this beautiful youth must be loved by his female relatives', the 1909 version speaks only of a vision 'of . . . sentiments infallibly entertained for this beautiful and amusing youth by the women of his house'. Of course, we easily surmise the nature of those sentiments, but it is of stylistic importance to note that they are no longer expressly *said* to be ones of love; 'sentiments infalliby entertained' is precisely the sort of phrase that a critic of James' later style might consider prolix; there seem to be too many words for the amount of information provided. Yet it is not that the information is less, but rather that it is more attenuated, and for characteristic esthetic reasons.

This trait is related to that of using general intensifiers without reference to what is being intensified: for example, Lord Mark's observation about Aunt Maud—that she is 'extraordinary'—but without specifying exactly what the adjective means.

D

8. OTHER SEMANTIC CATEGORIES

Psychological nouns form the most important and most easily
delineated category of intangibles in James, but certain other
semantic categories seem to emerge, even if classification is not
always entirely clear.

Though James is more than a 'society' novelist, much of what
he says has to do with 'society', and there are many words which
reflect a variety of social nuance.[1] They have the special flavour
of society small-talk; words like 'tone', 'note', 'contacts', the
ubiquitous 'type': Milly 'hadn't seen ["visions"] in connection...
with such a face as Lord Mark's, such eyes and such a voice, such
a tone and such a manner'; 'This easy ... jibe at her race was really
for her, on her new friend's part, the note of personal recognition
so far as she required it'; in New York Lord Mark's 'nameable
friends and his contrasted contacts had been numerous'; for
Milly, Lord Mark's 'type somehow, as by a life, a need, an intention of his own, insisted for him'. Compare 'line' (as in 'taking a
line'), 'air', 'manner', 'set' (a social group), 'fashion', 'form' (as in
'good form'), 'overture', 'affair', 'liberties' (what you 'take'),
'accessory' (they were 'surrounded ... with every English accessory') and 'relation' (Kate's 'type' is said to have 'sketched a
relation'). For Milly, Lord Mark is 'one of those cases she had
heard of at home—those characteristic cases of people in England
who concealed their play of mind so much more than they
showed it.'

---

[1] There is also a kind of 'society' implication of words like 'thing': the
narrator's reference to Waymarsh's complaints as 'these things' suggests a
stylish sloppiness of expression, a laziness permissible by *noblesse oblige*.

David Lodge has made an important contribution to our understanding
of these kinds of terms, and of James' later style generally, in 'Strether by
the River', in his *Language of Fiction* (London, 1966). Noting the importance

Less obviously 'social' words become so by the context. For example, 'pressure': Maria gently but procatively asks about Mrs. Newsome, and Strether seems to feel 'the pressure' of her questions. The word 'truth' might seem more resistant, but it too can be 'socialized': 'It had all gone so fast after this that Milly uttered but the truth nearest to hand in saying to the gentleman on her right . . . that she scarce even then knew where she was.' 'Passage' takes on the sense of 'conversation': 'Charlotte had but wanted the hint, and what was it but the hint, after all, that, during the so subdued but so ineffaceable passage in the breakfast room, she had seen her take.' 'Fortune' becomes 'social success': 'It almost appeared to Milly that their fortune had been unduly precipitated . . .'

It is not surprising that James should make use of 'society' words, but given his distaste for the subject—his famous unwillingness to name the product that Mr. Newsome had manufactured—it *is* surprising that he should so frequently use the language of practical affairs, of business, finance, the legal world. The reason, of course, is that most of the usages are metaphorical. Strether, than whom no one could be less a businessman, refers

of words like 'thing' ('*the* thing', 'the real thing', 'things') and 'wonderful' as well as trite metaphors like 'to be in the same boat with somebody', he has coined the apt phrase 'heightened cliché' (p. 196):

> It is a kind of in-group game which consists in managing to discuss, or at least to suggest, infinite complexities and discriminations in a vocabulary that is on the face of it remarkably impoverished, giving expressive force to platitudes and dead metaphors by devices of intonation, stress, placing, and repetition. . . . Clearly, James admires it as a form of linguistic virtuosity which has the social usefulness of enabling delicate subjects to be discussed publicly . . . ['Thing' is a] cliché which is heightened in Strether's use of it by being loaded with all his sensitive impressions.

Thus, the terms themselves would be hopelessly flat if it were not for the fact that they are used by subtle and refined minds, that is, the heightening is entirely due to the context of characters. Lodge finds the cliché 'wonderful', for example, to occur at least thirty-six times in *The Ambassadors*, noting: ' "Wonderful" becomes the supreme "in-group" word, which those who are "in" apply honorifically to each other and patronizingly to those who are "out". It is a word which blurs distinctions of value and opinion by its soothing flattery, its easy extravagance.' (p. 211) to his mission as 'business' on several occasions: '. . . the business he had come out on had not yet been so brought home to him as by the sight of the people around him'. Maggie sees that Charlotte's and Amerigo's 'business of social representation . . . was an affair of living always in harness'. There are also 'terms': when Maria permits Strether '. . . the purchase of a pair of gloves, the *terms* she made about it . . . were such as to fall upon a sensitive ear as a challenge to just imputations'. And 'attestations': 'Sharp to [Maggie] above all was the renewed attestation of her father's comprehensive acceptances.'

Another class of intangible words frequently used as subjects are nouns of time measurement, not only in the obvious way of saying 'a week passed', but more interestingly and character-istically as governing some human object. 'He had never expected —that was the truth of it—again to find himself young, and all the years and other things it had taken to make him so were exactly his present arithmetic.' Many of these constructions elim-inate the human actor completely: 'The prompt Paris morning struck its cheerful notes'; 'For a moment they stood confronted; then the moment placed her'; 'Amerigo was away from her again . . . but the hour was filled nevertheless with the effect of his nearness . . .'; '. . . the evening in Eaton Square might have passed for a demonstration all the more personal that the dinner had been on "intimate lines" '.

But the largest and most interesting class of intangible words outside the sphere of mental action is what Miss Krook refers to, under quotation marks, as 'logical' terms, terms for 'aspects, conditions and relations'. Her examples are 'relation', 'reci-procity', 'constatation', 'condition', 'categories', 'thing', 'appear-ances', 'implication', 'term', 'position', 'assumption', 'conse-quence'. To these can be added many others that occur even in my limited samples: 'phenomenon', 'subject', 'anomaly', 'nature', 'point', 'quantity', 'idea', 'case', 'topic', 'fact', 'combination', 'selection', 'cause', 'effect', 'sequel', 'result', 'occasion', 'object', 'demonstration', 'existence', 'concatenation', 'complement', 'form' 'opportunity', 'feature', 'theory', 'process', 'range', 'system', 'situation', 'position', 'state', 'quality', 'indication', 'connection', 'affinity', 'attribute', 'value', 'principle'. These hardly sound like words in a novel. What makes their usage odd and Jamesian is the way they fit into practical contexts (though an unsympathetic reader might complain that they are a way of making trivial things sound important). When James describes Lord Mark's activity in New York as 'his recollection of the whole mixed quantity', 'quantity' is, indeed, a high-powered way of referring to the balls, teas, concerts, and other rituals of high life at which he assisted. (Compare the change in *Roderick Hudson* from 'she struck me as a very intelligent girl' to 'she struck me as a decidedly positive quantity', or from 'Roderick began to talk about half a dozen statues' to 'Roderick began to talk of half a dozen plastic ideas'.) Or take that really heavyweight term, 'phenomenon'—Milly discovers that Lord Mark's conversational abilities may conceal something unpleasant: 'she had, on the spot, with her first plunge into the obscure depths of a society constituted from far back, encountered the interesting phenomenon of complicated, of possibly sinister motive'. The same word is used a bit later to describe the ambience at the dinner: 'appearances insisted and phenomena multiplied and words reached her from here and there like plashes of a slow, thick tide'. 'Phenomena' seems terribly high up the intellectual scale to describe the gestures and words, plate and silver of a mere dinner-party. Why does James avoid the tangible in a context which seems so appropriate to it? An answer might, in this case, at least, have some reference back to his concept of perception; the implication is that the splendour of the dinner-party was slightly confusing to Milly's senses. But there seems a better explanation for 'words' and even 'appearances' than for 'phenomena', which has so academic a sound, one so little suited to a debutante. These 'logical' words are applied to characters who would not actually use them (they are not evident in dialogue) and their use poses some interesting questions about James' treatment of point of view, about how—Lubbockians to the contrary—they presuppose a narrator interpreting the characters at such moments, rather than letting them interpret themselves.

It is even implied on occasion that a character's mind possesses or is controlled by or operates in terms of some whole set of 'logical' distinctions. There is reference, for example, to Kate Croy's 'system'. In the revised *Roderick Hudson*, Mary's 'habit' of consulting her guidebook becomes 'her system of concealing anxieties'. Maria Gostrey takes 'all [Strether's] categories by surprise'. On the very first page Strether's solitary landing is depicted as based upon 'a secret principle', and 'The principle of [Susan Stringham's] uneasiness was that Mrs. Lowder's life bristled for her with elements that she was really having to look at for the first time.' These are not only 'logical' but interpretative words, they are a narrator's words, not the words of the character. They are expository, rather than narrative, and they help to maintain a distance, often ironic, between character and narrator. They help to confirm the sense that despite all we know about them, the lives of Strether or Milly or Maggie are finally private and that at any moment they may retreat into them, become opaque, if that should suit James' purpose.

Some other 'logical' terms are worth looking at. Maggie pores over the 'chain of causes and consequences' that led to Charlotte's marriage to her father. Similarly, 'What perhaps most came out in the light of these concatenations was that it had been, for all the world, as if Charlotte had been "had in", as the servants always said of the extra help.' The vault from 'concatenation' to the slangy 'have in' is long and high but very Jamesian. Even more characteristic is the word 'relation'. Since much of James' fiction concerns relations between characters, or between characters and abstractions, or between abstractions and abstractions, even the smallest act—like tucking Waymarsh into bed—may find itself expressed by that word: 'Strether, with a kind coercive hand for it, assisted him to this consummation, and again found his own part in their relation suspiciously enlarged by the smaller touches of lowering the lamp and seeing to a sufficiency of blanket'.

There is an infinity of similar words. Strether's searching for something in his overcoat in front of Maria evokes an 'essence':

'the essence of the act was no more than the impulse to gain time'. The Prince's reappearance is described in words like 'form', 'action', 'opportunity', none further specified by adjectives: '. . . as the door opened again, she recognized, whatever the action, the form, at any rate, of a first opportunity'—Maggie's 'opportunity' itself is vague enough, let alone its 'form'. Even tangible objects evoke intangible expression: Strether compares Mrs. Newsome's ruff to Queen Elizabeth's, noting that 'it had after this, in truth, been his fancy that, as a consequence of that tenderness and an acceptance of the idea, the form of this special tribute to the "frill" had grown more marked'. Milly and Susan get into the swim of London: 'It wasn't then, as the prospect seemed to show, so difficult to get into the current, or to stand, at any rate, on the bank. It was easy to get near—if they *were* near, and yet the elements were different enough from any of her old elements, and positively rich and strange'; but what more can these 'elements' be than shopping, parties, balls, and visits?

A form often used by James is the pure adjective, without a suffix, as nominal. This, of course, is an abstraction in the purest sense of the word, the class of a single attribute over a population of individuals characterized only by joint possession of that attribute ('the poor' abstracts the attribute of being poor—and none other—from an otherwise heterogeneous group). James' fondness for the form is manifested by its frequent introduction into the revisions of the early novels; a clause like 'all this was but the painful complexity of genius' becomes in the 1909 version of *Roderick Hudson* 'a fine moral agitation, adding a zest to life, is the inevitable portion of those who, themselves unendowed, yet share romantically the pursuits of the inspired'. Similarly, 'His customary tolerance of circumstances' becomes 'His growing submission to the mere insidious actual'. The form is particularly characteristic where the adjective refers to things, rather than to people: Strether gives 'his afternoon to the immediate and the sensible'; Maria Gostrey is 'familiarly reminiscent of . . . the named, the numbered or the caricatured'; Kate and Merton settle 'on the short cut of the fantastic'. Such locutions could hardly be less tangible; beyond them there is nothing more than empty cover terms—what I shall call 'deictic nouns'—like 'something' and 'anything'.

James' secretary, Miss Bosanquet, reports his distaste for adjectives, attributing to him the remark that 'Adjectives are the sugar of literature and adverbs the salt'.[1] Of course, one way to get rid of adjectives is to nominalize them, to turn them into entities, to alter, in *Roderick Hudson*, 'These words of Rowland's were half impulsive, half deliberate' to 'These words . . . were half precipitation, half prudence'. Similarly there are numerous instances in the later style where the more obvious adjective-noun sequence has been rejected in favour of its transformed counter-part, the adjective, nominalized, followed by 'of' and the noun. Thus, instead of reference to a thing, which is more or less incidentally qualified, the reader is asked to focus on its quality, that is, the quality itself become a thing. We are not told that Strether's fancy was candid, but that he 'had a candour of fancy'. It is not that Strether had been sadly remorseful but that 'it had been the sadness of his remorse (that) . . .', not that he gave Waymarsh sufficient blankets, but rather 'a sufficiency of blanket' (in *Roderick Hudson*, 'the number of Bessie's blankets' is changed to 'the sufficiency of Bessie's bedclothes'). There are many other

---

[1] Because James is finally more concerned with *how* people do things than *what* they do, his partiality to adverbs, particularly manner adverbs, seems natural. It is a distinctive mark of his style to use unusual (foregrounding) -*ly* adverbs, for example, often modified by his own special intensifier 'all': '[Adam] might have been wishing to see how far she could go and where she would, all touchingly to him, arrive'. I find as many as eight of these adverbs on a single page of *The Golden Bowl*: 'really', 'deeply', 'exhaustively', 'pri-vately', 'truly', 'fairly', 'freely', 'provisionally'. In ten pages of the revision of *The American*, the later style adds eleven -*ly* adverbs: 'she said' for example, becomes 'she rather desperately said,' 'the marquis looked down at her' becomes 'the marquis hovered protectingly' (note ellipsis of the object); others are: 'simply', 'really', 'wonderfully', 'intimately', 'wonderingly', 'apparently', 'remarkably', 'presently', and 'strangely'. Cf. Gettman, pp. 281ff. Max Beerbohm had great fun with -*ly* adverbs intensified by *all* in his two parodies of James, 'The Mote in the Middle Distance' and 'The Guerdon' (see below).

examples of this stylistic habit: Little Bilham stands on a 'perched privacy' (not a private perch); in *The Wings of the Dove* we find not a charming demonstration of Kate's and Merton's need for each other but 'the charm of the demonstration'; Kate is not a cautious creature but 'a creature of precautions'; she has not a free fancy but 'freedom of fancy', not a superior 'humour' but 'superiority of "humour"', not graceful gaiety, but 'grace of gaiety'. In *The Golden Bowl* we have, instead of 'flat statement', a 'flatness of statement', instead of 'a various appeal' a 'variety of appeal', instead of 'bright high harmony' a 'brightness of high harmony', instead of 'her charming graceful curiosity' the 'charming grace of her curiosity', instead of 'this humble welcome', the 'humility of this welcome'. In the revised *Roderick Hudson*, 'in the bust there was nothing grossly satirical' is changed to 'the irony of portraiture was not gross'; and '. . . susceptibility to the influence of a beautiful woman' becomes '. . . susceptibility to their power to turn themselves "on" as creatures of subtlety and perversity'. Again and again we see the syntactic and semantic consequences of a preoccupation with an aspect of a thing, rather than the thing itself, and that aspect itself become a thing.

The importance attached to abstract nouns by James' style can also be measured by the amount of modification which they undergo. This seems particularly the case for nominalized forms: 'Strether felt that he was launched' could easily go without a modifier, indeed we might think of modification as superfluous. But 'Strether's feeling' almost demands some sort of adjectival rounding out; hence: 'Nothing could have been more odd than Strether's feeling that he had been launched.' Often the modifier is just the point: 'The principle I have just mentioned as operating had been, with the most newly disembarked of the two men, wholly instinctive.' For all James' preference for the adverb, he could not avoid the adjective; and the choice of a nominalization over its verbal counterpart often requires mention of a quality: 'the understanding . . . remained . . . sound', 'mixed with everything was the apprehension that . . .', 'the [self-] admonition . . . was . . . sharp', 'the exhibition was . . . not brilliant', 'the relation was . . . not the simplest', 'her consciousness of Mrs. Lowder's existence . . . had been of so recent and so sudden a birth', and so on. Expressing the quality of things, too, helps relieve the dryness of merely existential assertion: not simply a principle, but a 'secret principle', a 'happier device', a 'sharp sense', a 'recent vision', 'headlong hope', 'quiet evasion', 'double consciousness', 'old imaginations', 'perpetual reaction', 'proved sensibility', 'new perception', 'prime impression', 'immense little memory', and so on. If the narrator is 'forcing the reader to pay attention to James' primary objective—Strether's mental and subjective state',[1] that state is grasped through a set of qualified abstractions. The problem, however, is to keep the depiction of consciousness from sounding like a laundry list—item, a question about Waymarsh, item, the meaning of Maria Gostrey's attentions, etc., etc.

Mr. Watt has observed the preponderance in the late style of non-transitive verbs—copulas, passives, and intransitives. His explanation for a choice like 'Strether's first question was about . . .' over 'Strether first asked about . . .' is that the latter would 'merge Strether's consciousness into the narrative, and not isolate it for the reader's inspection'. This strikes me as exact, and the notion of 'inspection' crucial. The copula is the natural form for exhibiting things for inspection; we are not to be interested in what Strether does so much as in what he is like, inside even more than out. It must emerge, for example, that he is a man of several questions—some of which he hasn't even yet formulated— but that these will come to him in the course of the novel. The subject indeed is Strether's education, and one way to acquire an education is to ask questions. Since the reader is to be an inspector of mental contents, it is simpler, more direct, more economical to communicate with him in the expository rather than in the narrative mode. Actions are not there for their own sake but as interpreted—hence their frequent nominalization, since nouns are more easily itemized and catalogued than verbs. When we read that this was Strether's *first* question, not only do we infer

[1] Watt, p. 470.

that there are other questions to come, but that there is someone ordering and even, occasionally, evaluating Strether's actions. Strether, of course, cannot be imagined as saying to himself 'This is my first question'—that is one of the reasons why James so decisively rejected the first-person narrator. It is difficult to understand why critics insist so frequently that James is always and only an author who *shows*, not *tells*. A statement whose predication consists of copula and qualifier is by definition a statement of telling, and there are great numbers of these in the later style.

Indeed, one of James' motives for metaphor—so much increased in the later work—may very well have been his consciousness of the de-dramatizing effects of 'telling' about the inner life of his characters. The lively metaphoric predicate is often introduced to avoid the dull thud of the copula: 'this long ache might at last drop to rest'; 'this reasoning carried it [his scruple] off'; 'The earlier elements flushed into life again, the frequency, the intimacy, the high pitch of accompanying expression—appreciation, endearment, confidence'; 'This impression came out most for Maggie when . . . they had only themselves to regard'; 'his instinct . . . prompted him immediately to meet and match the difference'; 'This proved sensibility of the lady of Lancaster Gate performed . . . the office of a fine floating golddust.' I will have occasion to discuss James' metaphors at greater length, but these examples are sufficient to suggest something of his method of enlivening the representation of consciousness (and other intangibles) by means of figurative terms.

9. DEIXIS

For all their vagueness and generality the categories of nouns we have discussed so far do have some content, some independent reference, no matter how vague. But there is also a disposition in James' style towards a use of words which have no independent

content at all, only a deictic or pointing function, referring backward (or forward) to other words. Mr. Watt has discussed the
ubiquity of the neuter pronoun *it*, and I hope to add to that
discussion. But deictic nouns as well as pronouns are very
prevalent: almost empty words like 'thing' (including 'something',
'anything', 'nothing') abound, as well as 'item', 'matter', 'a great
deal', 'former', and 'latter', 'one', 'another', 'the other', and so on.
Within only a few pages of *The Ambassadors*, in which are described Maria's and Strether's dinner and evening at the theatre
(my italics): 'The manner in which Mrs. Newsome's throat *was*
encircled suddenly represented for him, in an alien order, almost
as many *things* as the manner in which Miss Gostrey's was'; 'The
connection . . . was . . . pathetic . . . and pathetic was doubtless,
in the conditions, the best *thing* it could possibly be'; 'All sorts
of *things* in fact now seemed to come over him, comparatively
few of which his chronicler can hope for space to mention'; 'The
publicity of the place was just, in the matter, for Strether, the rare,
strange *thing*'; '. . . in the drama, precisely, there was a bad
woman, in a yellow frock, who made a pleasant, weak, good-
looking young man, in perpetual evening dress, do the most
dreadful *things*'; 'It came up for him with Miss Gostrey that there
were *things* of which she would really perhaps, after all, have
heard; and she admitted when a little pressed that she was never
quite sure of what she heard as distinguished from *things* such as,
on occasions like the present, she only extravagantly guessed';
'*Something* in his manner showed it as quite pulling him up.'
The use of 'things' contributes measurably to the Jamesian sense
of plenitude without detail, but its vagueness is also, in a way,
fashionable, a kind of lazy society verbalism. There are other
words that have the same effect, for example 'elements', which
rarely means much more than 'things'. James apparently grew
so fond of this word that he was willing to sacrifice the relative
concreteness of metaphor to it: in the original version of *Roderick
Hudson* we read 'And yet he strongly felt her charm; the eddies
had a strange fascination'; in the revision, 'eddies' becomes
'elements'; 'And yet these elements in her were in themselves an

appeal to curiosity' (note the omission of personal reference). Similarly he changed '. . . if the response was vague, the satisfaction was great, and . . . Rowland after his second visit kept seeing a lurking reflection of this smile in the most unexpected places' to read 'if the response was vague, the satisfaction he drew from her mere colourless patience was great, and . . . he kept seeing the element itself reflected in the most unlikely surfaces, the most unexpected places'.

The barest deictic reference, of course, is by the pronoun *it*, and, as Mr. Watt has shown, James' style is excessively—sometimes bewilderingly—rich in that word. Sentences like the following are perfectly common: 'They made it continually greater, but that was what it had best be if it was to be anything at all, and he gave himself up . . . to feeling it grow.' There is no mercy for the poor reader who cannot remember what 'it' is.

It has several different functions in English, but the basic distinction is that between deictic and expletive. In the first, *it* stands for something in the nearer or farther environment. The reference may be to a specific word or words, or, as frequently in James, it may be vague—a whole phrase or sentence or paragraph or even a more or less implicit idea. The expletive *it*, on the other hand, is a mere anticipatory grammatical slot-filler; it occupies the position of grammatical subject when for some reason the real subject needs to be put in a later position, as when one says 'It's a nice day', rather than 'The day is nice'. James' heavy use of both deictic and expletive *it* is frequently a reflection of his preoccupation with intangibles—relations, aspects, conditions.

Vernon Lee has written very perceptively about James' use of the deictic pronouns. Her comment about a sentence in *The Ambassadors* ('what could it be . . . but the sense that Chad was . . . as good as he thought') is worth quoting: '. . . the thing we are watching with Strether, almost hunting, indeed, is not a human being nor an animal, neither is it a locality we are trying to discover; not even a concrete peculiarity we want to run to ground; it is the most elusive of psychological abstractions: a

force, a *belief*, in other words an intellectual residum of experience.'[1]
What helps to make this 'thing' a thing is precisely to refer to it
as an 'it'. It is the pronoun which enables James to make so much
of 'sense', establishing it as grammatical subject rather than
predicate verb of the question, instead of saying merely that
Strether sensed that Chad was as good as he thought.

But we cannot grasp the full significance of this trait without
considering its widespread occurrence: statistics again are necessary. In the same samples discussed above, I find that as many as
fifteen per cent of grammatical subjects are deictic pronouns
(in *The Wings of the Dove*). Compared to the other writers, James
uses deictic pronouns as subjects three, four, even seven times
as often as the others (Forster and Conrad). Again *The American*
is more like the other novelists' style; in comparison deictic pronouns as subjects in the sample from *The Portrait of a Lady* are
six times more numerous, illustrating once more that its affinity
with James' later style is considerably greater than that of *The
American*.

The use of deictic pronouns to replace abstractions—intangible
nouns, whole clauses and sentences, and even vaguer referents—
is a profound confirmation of their existence. For they are not
merely being referred to; they are being converted—by the very
grammar—into things, entities, as substantial as any character.
As Vernon Lee notes, the consequence is almost 'a sort of
personification'.

Consider the following passage from *The Wings of the Dove*
(neuter pronouns referring to intangibles are italicized):

Kate Croy, fine but friendly, looked over at her [Milly] as really with a
guess at Lord Mark's effect on her. If she could guess this effect what
then did she know about *it* and in what degree had she felt *it* herself?
Did *that* represent, as between them, anything particular, and should
she have to count with them as duplicating, as intensifying by a mutual
intelligence, the relation into *which* she was sinking? Nothing was so
odd as that she should have to recognize so quickly in each of these
glimpses of an instant the various signs of a relation; and this anomaly

[1] Lee, p. 244.

itself, had she had more time to give to *it*, might well, might almost
terribly have suggested to her that her doom was to live fast. *It* was
clearly a question of the short run and the consciousness proportion-
ately crowded.

These were immense excursions for the spirit of a young person at
Mrs. Lowder's mere dinner-party; but what was so significant and so
admonitory as the fact of *their* being possible? What could *they* have
been but just a part, already, of the crowded consciousness? And . . .
it was just a part that while this process went forward our young lady
alighted, came back, taking up her destiny again as if she had been
able by a wave or two of her wings to place herself briefly in sight of
an alternative to *it*. Whatever *it* was *it* had showed in this brief interval
as better than the alternative; and *it* now presented *itself* altogether in
the image and in the place in *which* she had left *it*. The image was *that*
of her being, as Lord Mark had declared, a success. *That* depended
more or less of course on the idea of the thing—into *which* at present,
however, she wouldn't go.

One is almost overwhelmed by the pronouns and other deictic
elements and slightly aghast at the problem of figuring out their
references;[1] it takes careful reading to determine that 'she' in the

---

[1] In his able dissertation, *Henry James: The Late and Early Styles* (Uni-
versity of Michigan, 1953), pp. 32, 36, Leo Hendrick notes that in comparative
samples of 3,000 words taken from early and late texts, the number of personal pronouns increases by more than a third, from 158 to 217. His explanation for this increase is that 'The thoughts of self-conscious characters are
mostly of self; and self can hardly be expressed except with personal pronouns.' This explains an increase in reflexive pronouns, perhaps, but not
necessarily the others. My own small investigation of the revision of *The
American* showed as many as fifteen changes from the noun (e.g. 'Newman')
to the pronoun ('he') in eleven pages, and none of these were reflexives.
James' preference for the pronoun in these cases—mostly subject positions—
seems simply an adherence to the general compositional rule that a name or
common noun need only be introduced when the person (or thing) referred
to has changed. But this principle is often violated; James is quite ready to
risk confusing the reader by using *he* where there are two men, *she* where
there are two women, or *they* where there are more than two people, as in the
extensive passage quoted above.

R. W. Short also discusses ambiguity of pronoun reference: see p. 81 of
'The Sentence Structure of Henry James'.

second sentence is Kate and not Milly, but in the third sentence
Milly and not Kate, and that 'them' in the third sentence is Kate
and Lord Mark, not Milly and Lord Mark. And all the other *its*,
thats, *whiches* and deictic nouns like *thing* and *alternative* are not
much easier to cope with.

Vernon Lee defends this aspect of James' style on rhetorical
grounds, that is, in terms of the author-reader relationship. James,
she felt, practised a kind of natural selection among readers; the
pronouns were simply part of the obstacle course. His reader
'must remember what the pronoun stands for . . . the Reader will
have to be, spontaneously, at full cock of attention, a person
accustomed to bear things in mind, to carry on a meaning from
sentence to sentence, to think in abbreviations; in other words he
will have to be an intellectual, as distinguished from an impulsive
or *imageful* person.'[1] One might add that the use of personal pronouns instead of proper names heightens the sense of intimacy
and intense engagement with the characters, draws the reader
closer to them, more completely into their network of relations.

But we are particularly interested in the neuter pronoun,
especially where it replaces some intangible referent. The passage
above gives some indication of the prevalence of that reference.
In the second sentence 'it' refers back to the intangible 'effect'.
That 'effect' is subtle—it is the set of Milly's reactions to Lord
Mark's appearance, personality, 'line', but only her visible
reactions, only what she can allow herself to reveal at a sedate
dinner party. (That it's all Milly's speculation is underlined by the
hypothetical elements 'as really with' and 'if'.) Calling the effect
'it' makes it a matter to be dealt with, grants it status as a genuine
counter in the game. The pronoun is one more way of underlining

[1] p. 244. Booth has found a passage in James' early essay 'The Novels of
George Eliot' (*The Atlantic Monthly*, October, 1866) which shows that
'making the reader' was a completely conscious part of his fictional theory
and method: the author ' "makes his reader very much as he makes his
character".' (Booth, p. 49) Booth adds: 'James is not thinking here simply
of giving the reader a sense of his own cleverness. He is making his readers
by forcing them onto a level of alertness that will allow for his most subtle
effects.' (p. 302)

the importance of the intangibles, of making them the subject of the discourse even more than the characters who rummage or flounder among them.

The reference of 'that' in the third sentence is even vaguer. The question raises the first hint of an undercover communication between the 'others', the English, that Milly can only guess at. What is confusing is that 'that' might seem to refer again to 'effect', on the principle, cited above, of the unchanging reference of pronouns. But clearly it does not. Rather, it refers to the whole phenomenon: the surmise that Kate is strangely knowledgeable about Lord Mark's effect on her; that as a consequence Kate must know Lord Mark rather intimately (the question 'Did that represent . . . anything particular', is rhetorical; the answer is 'Of course it did'); and that Kate has probably made a pretty shrewd reading of Milly in the short time they have been together. 'That' says something of the sort, but in a vague way, a way which perhaps mirrors Milly's uncertainty about the whole relationship.

'It' in the fourth sentence refers back to 'anomaly', which in turn refers back to the oddness of Milly's recognizing so quickly 'the various signs of a relation'. The precise nature of that relation —as so often in James—is not given; it is not even clear whether the relation is between Milly and Lord Mark, or between Kate and Lord Mark, or between Kate and Milly, or among all three. We probably are meant to choose the first, since Milly is described as 'sinking' into it, but we don't do so with complete confidence. At any rate, we are left to wonder at the delicacies of a morality in which mere conversation with a dinner partner (whom, after all, one did not pick) should expose a woman to the ominous Victorian accusation of 'living fast' (although 'live fast' may not mean 'sink into iniquity' but simply 'experience everything so soon'—going back to her 'quick recognition'). The whole thing is hyperbolic, ironic and vague in the typically Jamesian manner.

'It' and 'these', in the fifth and sixth sentences, are grammatically more complex. In both cases there is a double reference, both backward (deictic) and forward (expletive). These are expletives to the extent that the sentences are transformations of

E

underlying structures like 'The question was clearly of the short run' and 'These excursions were immense', in both cases the pronouns merely anticipating a later noun. But there are also deictic possibilities, since 'it' could refer to the whole business of Milly's sinking into a relation with Lord Mark and Kate's close observation of the process, and 'these' to the thoughts represented in sentences two through five—'these [thoughts] were immense excursions'. The semantic consequences are minor enough, but it seems useful to note that James is getting two for one, that the use of the pronouns, far from being loose, actually unifies these sentences in a rhetorically persuasive way. The conversion of 'these' of sentence six into the genitive 'their' and into 'they' as the subject of sentence seven further heightens the sense of the unity and importance of the abstractions, of these ruminatings and 'excursions'. As before, the deictic notation makes the abstraction familiar, something to be borne in mind as it is turned around and around in succeeding grammatical facets. Vernon Lee refers to the process as 'circling': 'There is . . . an extraordinary circling round these pronouns. I feel that, had they been *nouns*, they would have undergone some transformation [not grammatical transformation, obviously; perhaps replacement by synonyms or other words], not remained this selfsame something we circle about. Circle about and among; for we penetrate between them (one almost forgets what *they* really are, feeling *them* merely as something with which one is playing some game— pawns? draughts? or rather adversaries?), finding them now as a nominative, now a possessive, now a dative. It is noteworthy that this shifting of the *case* of these pronouns gives the sentence an air of movement. . . .'[1] One *almost* forgets, but not really, if he is reading well, since to do so would be to lose the thread of the story. But I would not deny that they convey movement and have an almost hypnotic effect.

The 'it' which is the subject of the next sentence, the eighth, is expletive rather than deictic, anticipating the entire following *that*-clause, presumably *another* part of the crowded consciousness,

[1] pp. 243–4.

an addition to the 'excursions' discussed above. (Note that it is 'the crowded consciousness', not 'her crowded consciousness'.) There follows another instance of deixis, by a noun (that is, elegant variation): 'process' points back to 'excursions', making a chain of reference. The sentence ends with an 'it' which vaults us backward a distance of twenty-five words, to 'destiny'; the effort of recall, again, seems to support the importance of the thing as thing. Having retrieved 'destiny', James examines it at close quarters in the ninth sentence: 'whatever it was it had showed . . . as better than the alternative . . .' again making a good deal of the abstraction by turning it about, peering at it from this side and that. And of course 'alternative' also is deictic; it has no real semantic content since its meaning, 'another destiny', exists only in opposition to this destiny. The palpability of 'destiny' is further increased by the gratuitous reflexive predicate of the next clause: 'it now presented itself. . . .' The spatial metaphor continued the objectification: 'it' is in an 'image' and in a 'place in which she had left it'. The 'that' of sentence ten is an anticipatory deixis for 'The image was of her being . . .' 'That' is grammatically superfluous, stylistically another case of entitization—her being something, a 'that', becomes a kind of thing in itself.

The last sentence contains a virtual crescendo of deixis. The subject, 'that', must refer not to 'success' tout court but to a more conjectural form—'whether or not she was a success', which depends on 'the idea of the thing'—an abstracted, deictic reference to another abstraction, 'the thing' necessarily referring back to 'her being a success', but this time to the term itself, its definition, with the strong hint that there are certain kinds of 'successes' that Milly would not care to be. Again we have the effect of making much of the thing by heavy grammatical business, 'it' being converted into the relative pronoun 'which' as object of a prepositional phrase stylistically anticipating its head.

Looking back over the passage we note not only the extreme, even exaggerated prevalence of deixis, but also, in every case, that reference is back to abstractions. Thus deictics form a kind of secondary level of abstraction underlining the primary. As any delver into late James knows, this kind of thing is not unusual; it can go on for pages on end. Nor is it limited to original writing in the late style; there are many instances in the revisions to show that James increasingly chose to express himself this way. For example, what was originally, in *Roderick Hudson*, 'on the whole Roderick was not a generous fellow, and he [Rowland] was far from having ceased to believe him' is changed to 'on the whole the values in such a spirit were not much larger than the voids, and he was far from having ceased to believe in it . . .' Because 'Roderick' becomes 'spirit', 'him' must become 'it', and it takes an extra moment for the reader to remember to what, or rather to whom that 'it' ultimately refers. Similarly, the already difficult sentence 'Rowland found . . . a perfect response to his prevision that to live in Rome was an education to the sense and the imagination, but he sometimes wondered whether this were not a questionable gain in case of one's not being prepared to subside into soft dilettantism' is made more so by changing the last phrase to read 'prepared to ask no more consciousness than they', where 'they' (I think!) refers back to 'sense' and 'imagination'— a distance of twenty-seven words.

Given infinite evidence of James' artistry, it would be folly to conclude that these floods of *its*, *thats*, *theses*, *thoses*, and *whiches*, and a variety of deictic nouns like 'thing', 'one', and 'matter' are the products of inadvertent clumsiness, marks of the kind of ineptness that undermines the writing of college freshmen. James' practice clearly violates the copybook rules about 'clarity' of pronominal reference, yet its effect seems brilliant. Since the deictics are so seriously and so ably used, it is clearly the task of stylistics to determine their quality, to observe their esthetic effect and to surmise an 'intention'. And to me the clearest association is with James' general abstractness or intangibility.

Deixis is usually defined as a backward reference, and in most cases the referent does physically precede the pronoun or other deictic element. But anticipatory deixis is also possible, and in James not infrequent. Perhaps most interesting—and slightly unEnglish, the French influence seeming likely—is what could be called 'appositive deixis', a pronoun or the like being given first, anticipating the real subject, which follows in apposition. The first sentence of *The Wings of the Dove* contains this structure: 'She waited, Kate Croy, for her father to come in . . .' In Chapter V of *The Ambassadors* alone there are no less than six instances with neuter forms, three of them referring to intangible nouns: 'It would serve, this spur to his spirit, he reflected . . . as pausing at the top of the street, he looked up and down the great foreign avenue, it would serve to begin business with' ('this spur' refers back to the 'sense of injury' Strether felt at not receiving mail); 'It filled for him, this tone of hers, all the air'; and 'They had proved, successively, these impressions—all of Musette and Francine, but Musette and Francine vulgarized by the larger evolution of the type—irresistibly sharp'. The unusual positioning of these deictic forms heightens, by a syntactic 'foregrounding', the entitization of the intangibles. Again, there is a sense of 'making much of', of asserting that these abstractions have not become grammatical and logical subjects by accident but by careful design, and that that design is of real importance to the tale, something to be mulled over.

As shown above, *it*-constructions occur occasionally that are both deictic and expletive: '[Waymarsh] struck his visitor as extremely, as almost willfully, uncomfortable; yet what had this been for Strether, from that first glimpse of him disconcerted on the porch of the hotel, but the predominant note? It was a discomfort that was in a manner contagious, as well as also, in a manner, inconsequent and unfounded. . . .' On the one hand, 'it' refers back to 'uncomfortable' (it is awkward but not impossible to say 'His uncomfortableness was a discomfort that . . .'). On the other, it is a simple filler for the real subject, 'discomfort', since we can just as easily say 'The discomfort was in a manner contagious'. This double grammar, this slight uncertainty about 'it', makes it and its referent 'loom' the more. *It* in double function is often introduced into the revised version of *Roderick Hudson*. For example, in the sentences 'Rowland had already been sensible of something in this young lady's [Christina's] tone which he would have

called a want of veracity, and this epitome of her religious experience failed to strike him as absolutely historical. But the trait
was not disagreeable . . .', James replaces 'the trait was not
disagreeable' with 'it was no disfiguring mask'. 'It' can refer back
either to a previous noun—to 'want of veracity' (which has been
changed to 'easy use of her imagination') or to 'this epitome of
her religious experience'—or it can anticipate a construction
whose unelliptical expression would be 'But it was no disfiguring
mask that she wore', or the like.

10. CLEFT SENTENCES AND RELATED FORMS

There is another kind of 'copying' or repetition of the subject
(or object) which is even commoner in James' late style and no
less evocative of the sense of intangibility, namely what is now
often called the 'cleft sentence' structure. The 'clefting' transformation performs either of the following two operations:
either it places *what* before the noun phrase and *be* between the
verb and its object: 'Coughs cause disease'→'What coughs cause
is disease'; or it replaces the subject with *what* and adds the subject
at the end, after an inserted *be*: 'Coughs cause disease'→'What
causes disease is coughs'.[1]

---

[1] This is something of a simplification. See R. A. Jacobs and P. S. Rosenbaum, *English Transformational Grammar* (Waltham, Mass., 1968), pp. 39–40,
for a more exact formulation. The second transformation but not the first
works where the original object is human: 'What angered me was his tone',
but not *'What his tone angered was me', because *what* cannot be used to
'question' a human noun, and a parallel use of *who* has simply not developed
in English. The reverse situation holds when the subject is human and the
object non-human: we can say 'What John kicked was the dog' but not
'What (or who) kicked the dog was John.' So if *both* nouns are human, the
cleft-sentence transformation is impossible: neither *'What (whom) John
kissed was Mary' nor *'What (who) kissed Mary was John.' But there is
another kind of cleft-sentence which may work with humans, namely, that

Naturally, other transformations may complicate the construction, and one of the sources of syntactic complexity in James is precisely such an accumulation: from *The Golden Bowl*, '. . . what perhaps most came out in the light of these concatenations was that it had been, for all the world, as if Charlotte had been "had in".' Here we have the second kind of *what*-cleft-sentence transformation, where the subject and verb are inverted, after the deletion of *it*. (Note that with intransitive verbs only the extraposed form can exist without 'clefting': we can say 'It came out in the light of these concatenations that it had been as if Charlotte had been "had in",' which is a product of the extraposition transformation and non-deletion of *it*; but we can hardly say 'That it had been as if Charlotte had been "had in" came out in the light of these concatenations'. In general, *it* is inserted if the subject would otherwise be top-heavy.)

The cleft sentence is typically used to highlight the element anticipated by *what* (or *it*): *disease* in 'What coughs cause is disease' and *coughs* in 'what causes disease is coughs'. Thus the locution occurs frequently for special emphasis: 'What I like is cheese' tells us not only that I like cheese but that that indeed is the certain thing in the universe of foodstuffs that claims any preference. The emphasis often has an excluding implication: 'I like a lot of things but what I especially like is . . .' or 'There are lots of things to like; what I like is . . .'

The following is a description of Waymarsh: 'The head was bigger, the eyes finer, than they need have been for the career; but that only meant, after all, that the career was itself expressive. What it expressed at midnight in the gas-glaring bedroom at Chester was that the subject of it had, at the end of years, barely escaped, by flight in time, a general nervous collapse.' The second sentence is logically (if not grammatically) the object of the adjective 'expressive' which is repeated as the verb 'expressed'. What effects are gained by phrasing it as a cleft sentence rather than more straightforwardly, 'It expressed . . . that the subject . . .'

with *it* before the subject and a relative pronoun after: 'It was Mary who kissed John' ('it is coughs that cause disease').

etc.? The power and importance of the word 'express' is heightened by 'what'; what is said is 'Yes, the career did indeed express a something, a "what" '. Further, the focus on the result at the very outset allows it to be held in suspense until after the evocation of the scene—'at midnight, in the gas-glaring bedroom at Chester'. We can tolerate the intrusive stage-setting since our course has been so firmly set by the opening *what*. Similarly, in 'When, in a quarter of an hour, he [Strether] came down, what his hostess [Miss Gostrey] saw, what she might have taken in with a vision kindly adjusted, was the lean, slightly loose figure of a man of the middle height . . .', it is the object that is questioned, helping us hold in mind that a something has indeed been seen, Maria, of course, being a person whom we must assume to be constantly 'seeing', 'taking things in'. The things seen will be identified quickly enough, so that for the moment we may delve into the subtleties of the possible manners of seeing—this was seeing 'with a vision kindly adjusted'. Note too that though the object in fact turns out to be quite concrete—poor old Strether—*what* itself is so general as to set us up for any possibility, even the most intangible. Maria could as easily have 'seen' an abstraction or a proposition. Thus, even human beings can be made to seem more abstract by being placed in a syntax which could as easily anticipate abstract nouns.

Where the 'questioned' noun is already intangible, the cleft-construction makes it more so: 'What carried him [Strether] hither and yon was an admirable theory that nothing he could do would not be in some manner related to what he fundamentally had on hand . . .'; or a *that*-clause: 'What befell, however, was that even while she [Maggie] thus waited she felt herself present at a process taking place . . .'; or an infinitive phrase: '. . . what she [Milly] had in fact done was to renew again her effect of showing herself to its possessor [Kate] as conjoined with Lord Mark for some interested view of it'.

Consider the following: Lord Mark has managed, in the face of a retort of Milly's, to 'assure her of his consideration. She wondered how he had done it, for he had neither apologized nor protested. She said to herself, at any rate, that he had led her on; and what was most odd was the question by which he had done so.' Is 'most' a real superlative or only an intensifier? Paraphrases like 'The question by which he had done so was most odd' or 'It was most odd how he had done so' preserve only the sense of general intensification, 'most' being simply a synonym for 'very'. The cleft construction may mean only that, but it may also imply that there were a variety of other odd things in Lord Mark's behaviour. The sense of 'plenitude' (as we see elsewhere) is very important in James: 'Lord Mark said and did a lot of odd things but the oddest was the question . . .' ('If I had time, dear reader, I could give you ever so many more examples'). The ambiguity and vagueness are 'rich'; there are heavy implications in the net of reasoning, in the numerous set of categorizations and classifications which is James' world.

The cleft *what*-construction may be very useful in helping to fuse the intangible with the concretely metaphorical: 'What had come as straight to him as a ball in a well-played game—and caught, moreover, not less neatly—was just the air, in the person of his friend [Maria], of having seen and chosen, the air of achieved possession of these vague qualities and quantities that figured to him, collectively, as the advantage snatched from lucky chances.' Here it is the subject—the 'air'—which is 'questioned', the 'what' permitting James to delay its complex specification so that he may express leisurely, in a metaphor, the manner of acquisition. It seems entirely appropriate, in a novel about an education, that the *manner* should be given primacy in the syntax. The way in which Strether learns something is the important thing; what he learns is secondary, since he is bound to learn a great deal about a lot of things before he is finished. The same delaying of the subject, of course, could have been achieved with the expletive *it*—'It had come to him straight as a ball in a well-played game that . . .' But *it* does not convey so strongly the hint that it was predictable that something should indeed come to him, and that our part is rather to note its arrival than to be surprised by its content. It is as if James were saying, 'You are, of course, dear and so knowledgeable reader, correctly anticipating that Strether, this sensitive instrument, would 'catch' something, make some inference about Maria; what in fact *had* come as straight to him as a ball . . . was . . .' The cleft construction presupposes a reader capable, ready, indeed eager, to make such predictions. The sense of inevitability is, if anything, more exaggerated when the *what* part of the construction is delayed to the predicate: 'The amusement, at all events, of a civilisation . . . was what . . . she [Maria] appeared distinctly to promise' ('Naturally Maria could be expected to promise something . . .'); or 'Surprise, it was true, was not on the other hand what the eyes of Strether's friend most showed him. . .' ('They would, of course, in any case, show him *something*').

But the cleft sentence says even more. Since its predicate in every case is the copula, whatever action may have been conveyed by the original verb is eliminated, and the construction becomes a categorization, or, to anticipate what I shall say later, an illustration. The esthetic effect is not that something has happened, but that that happening, now a thing, an *item*, can be considered, handled, categorized. And the preference of *what* over *it* seems to suggest that some effort has been exerted to find the real issues and reasons. It is a way of asserting the authority and trustworthiness of the narrator, since it implies that he really has searched about and is ready to offer you the very thing—among the mass of background details—that you are to know.

Though the number of cleft sentences in the sample may seem relatively small, it represents a heavy usage compared to the styles of the other novels I have examined. In all the passages of comparable length from Forster, Gissing, Butler, and Conrad, I found only a single instance of either *what*- or *it*-clefting, while there are as many as six *what*-clefts alone in the selection from *The Golden Bowl*.

The anticipatory construction with *it*-expletive is of course more frequent. But there are a sufficient number of *what*-clause subjects to make them clearly distinctive of James. They form the more unusual and therefore more highlighted or foregrounded way of indicating that a sentence, that is, a proposition, is in fact the subject of the predication, with the consequent esthetic effects suggested above.

What-cleft sentences easily become awkward, so James often has recourse to the *it* expletive. The use of *it* in a cleft is a weaker and less pointed effect than *what*: 'It is coughs that cause colds' does not imply the certainty, the focus or selection against a background of reference quite so strongly as 'What causes colds are coughs'. The difference between 'What came as straight as a ball in a well-played game is . . .' and 'It came to him straight as a ball . . . that' has already been discussed. Still there is a modicum of emphasis or prior-reference in the *it*-cleft, since 'It is coughs that cause colds' still says more than 'Coughs cause colds'.

Here are some Jamesian examples of the *it*-cleft used to question the subject: 'It was the former [the 'voice of Milrose'] . . . that was most in the real tradition'; 'It was the soreness of his remorse that the child had . . . not really been dull . . .'; 'It was the handsome girl alone, of his own species and his own society, who had made him feel uncertain'. For some reason, the *it*-cleft, like the *what*-cleft, occurs most frequently in the selection from *The Golden Bowl*: 'It was the very sense of the stage and the footlights that kept her up, made her rise higher; just as it was the sense of action that logically involved some platform . . .'; 'It was they themselves who were arranged'; 'In this other scene it was Lady Castledean who was determinant . . .'

But it is not only the nouns that are 'copied' by cleft-*it* in James. One of his more idiosyncratic traits is to use it to emphasize modificational elements, and more particularly, adverbial elements: '. . . it was here she [Maria] presently checked him with a question'; or with an inversion: 'Then it was that the dismissed vision of Amerigo, that evening . . . then it was that this immense little memory gave out its full power.' Even more frequent is the copying of prepositional phrases: 'It wasn't till after he had spoken that he became aware of how much there had been in him of response'; 'Under this particular impression it was that everything in Maggie most melted and went to pieces'; 'It was in the mitigated midnight of these approximations that she had made out the promise of her dawn'; 'It was not from her that they took their cue . . . but from each other . . .'; 'It was with Waymarsh he should have shared it . . .'; 'It was for Maggie to wonder, at present, if she had been sincere about their going . . .' These are of particular interest to us since their function is to point up relationships, rather than objects, intangibles rather then tangibles.

That brings me to James' use of sentences as nouns, particularly as subjects of other sentences, and of *it* as an expletive introducing such structures. This construction, too, is by definition more intangible than what it replaces. No matter how concrete the included sentence in itself, embedding it makes the whole new sentence more abstract. If we convert 'This chair is low' into 'That this chair is low is unnecessary' or 'This chair's being low is unnecessary', or 'For this chair to be low is unnecessary', we introduce a propositional logic which transfers the chair from the realm of the senses to that of the intellect. Our minds are removed from the concrete object to some proposition about it.

Sentences of this kind are handled in contemporary grammar as transforms of sentences with expletives as subjects.[1] Any noun may optionally be followed by a sentence which modifies it. The sentence is connected to the noun by a 'complementizer', a relative pronoun or conjunctive *that*: 'The man who came is here', 'The news that you are here is welcome'. Since in this kind of grammar every noun phrase must have a head, sentences like 'That you are here is welcome news' must modify some deleted subject, some *it* in the deep structure. *It* may or may not be deleted by a later transformation; deletion gives 'That you are here is welcome news'; non-deletion and the so-called 'extra-position transformation' gives 'It is welcome news that you are here'.

That-clauses as subjects—produced by deletion of *it*—are comparatively rare in the passages under consideration, although my impression is that they must be fairly frequent in James' prose.

[1] See Jacobs and Rosenbaum, chapters 7, 20, and 21 for a simple statement. Cf. also D. Terence Langendoen, 'The Syntax of the English Expletive "It" ', *Georgetown Monograph in Languages and Linguistics* (1966), pp. 207ff.

It is interesting that in the two instances that turn up in the selections from *The Ambassadors*, the subject gets repeated by a deictic element, almost as if apologetically for the top-heavy effect: 'That the memory of the vow of his youth should, in order to throb again, have had to wait for this last, as he felt it, of all his accidents—that was surely proof enough of how his conscience had been encumbered'.

Sentences like 'What happened is welcome news' are similarly derived. The chief difference is that where *that* simply introduces the clause-as-subject, *what* is both conjunction and subject: the sentence is derived from a deep structure containing the two sentences 'It happened' and 'It is welcome news', to which are applied transformations deleting the second *it* and converting the first to *what*. If *what* is the object, as in 'What you said was welcome news', we must presume the deep structures 'You said it' and 'It was welcome news', in which case we have not only a deletion of the second *it* and a conversion of the first to *what*, but also a transposition of *what* to initial position. *What* in such cases—unlike cleft sentences—does not anticipate a noun in the same construction. Its reference must be found in the outside context, so it is deictic rather than expletive. For example, in 'What causes diseases was discussed', *What* remains unidentified until we are provided with more context or can supply it from our own life experience. From *The Golden Bowl*, 'What [Prince Amerigo] wanted was put to the proof'; from *The Ambassadors*, 'What seemed all surface one moment seemed all depth the next'. In such cases, *what* is no more concrete than a deictic noun like *something*. Other interrogatives can be used: 'Why his [Lord Mark's] judgment so mattered remained to be seen.' The interesting and unusual thing in James' style is that cleft *what*-constructions outnumber non-cleft *what*-constructions of this sort by over six to one. It is clear that the use of a clause as subject is chiefly, with James, a device for controlling and directing our attention in the ways described above, a device like others for emphasizing the real existence and importance of announced intangibles—ideas, qualities, and propositions.

11. EXPLETIVE *IT*

James is a heavier user of the expletive *it* as subject than any of
the other authors. In the passage from *The Wings of the Dove*,
for example, twenty-four instances, or 8 per cent, of the subjects
of main clauses are expletive-*its*, while Forster employs only 4 per
cent, Gissing 1 per cent, Butler 4 per cent, and Conrad 5 per cent.
Again, *The Portrait of a Lady* is far in advance of *The American*
on the way to the later style, showing half again as many instances
as the earlier novel.

James' favourite expletive construction is with the adjective,
either alone—'It was positively droll to him that he should
already have Maria Gostrey, whoever she was . . . in a place of
safe keeping'; 'It was . . . open to her [Milly] that his line was to be
clever'—or with a noun: 'It made . . . the third time since his
[Amerigo's] return that he had drawn her to his breast'; 'It was
no light matter . . . that the very effect of his confusion should
make him again prevaricate.' Sometimes a noun clearly replaces a
counterpart adjective: 'It was a mercy . . . that their fancies jumped
together' (for 'merciful'); 'it was a wonder . . . that he didn't hate
her more' (for 'wonderful'). Other nouns may occur, in more or
less idiomatic function: '. . . it was no fault of the girl's if the good
lady had not now appeared in a peaked hat . . .' Or the noun
may be a gerund: '. . . it would be going too far to say that he was
ashamed of them'. Occasionally, James used even adverbs: 'It
was still, for her [Maggie], that she had positively something to
do'.

More common is the expletive with a prepositional phrase, in
either adjectival or adverbial function: 'It was already upon him,
even at that distance, that Mr. Waymarsh was for *his* part joyless';
'It wasn't till after he had spoken that he became aware of how
much there had been in him of response'; '. . . hadn't it been

distinctly on the ground that he *was* tired that his wonderful friends at home had so felt for him and so contrived?'; '... of what service was it to find himself making out after a moment that the quality ... was probably ... a case of distinction?' The intangibility of these constructions is obvious, particularly spatial-metaphorical ones like 'to be upon him', and 'to be on the ground that'.

Often in James *it is* introduces a whole clause beginning with *as if*. On a single page of *The Ambassadors* we find as many as three instances: '[Maria] paused while our friend took in these things, and it was as if a good deal of talk had already passed'; 'It was almost as if she had been in possession and received him as a guest'; 'It was as if this personage ['the lady in the glass cage' in the hotel] had seen herself instantly superseded'. The importance to James of his locution (which occurs only once in all the eight hundred sentences by the other novelists) cannot be overestimated. It is the means by which the character's imagination is opened to speculation, but without suggestions of idle fantasizing. In this passage, Strether is trying to figure out what delightful thing may be happening to him; he needs to conjecture, and the instrument of conjecture is *as if*. It is a safe instrument, since no one—neither Strether nor his interpreter—is necessarily comitted to it as the exact state of things. It was as if Maria were a hostess receiving him, that's the way she made him feel: the focus is directly upon Strether's feeling of the moment, the surface of his mind (as Lubbock puts it), not upon its depths. In fact, the narrator is not even asserting that these were Strether's very words, that it was Strether who was metaphorizing; there is a delicate but clear distance suggested, and the authority for the simile is kept vague. That was how the situation 'felt' according to the *narrator*, whether or not the character would have expressed it in those terms.[1]

[1] Wayne Booth has shown how modern 'objective' novelists manage to 'reap all the benefits' of direct commentary on action and character by conjecturing freely about mere surface appearances, as if saying that it *looked* so is not 'really' the same as saying it *was* so. He notes particularly how

Examples of *as if* are even more frequent in *The Wings of the Dove*: 'It was almost at present as if [Milly's] poor prevision [of the banquet, of her socializing in London] had been rebuked by the majesty—she could scarcely call it less—of the event . . .' It provides a way of handling Milly's wonder at Aunt Maud's glorious welcome: 'She had thus engaged them to dine but two days later . . . It was as if she really cared for them . . .' Or of her interested but slightly repelled reaction to Lord Mark's 'line': ' "You'll notice," he pleasantly wound up, "that I've confidence in you." "Why shouldn't you have?" Milly asked, observing in this, as she thought, a fine, though for such a man, a surprisingly artless, fatuity. It was as if there might have been a question of her falsifying for the sake of her own show.' But the heaviest occurrence of the locution is in the sample from *The Golden Bowl* where there are no less than six instances. It is the perfect medium of Maggie's soul struggle: 'It was as if for her the opportunity had depended on his look—and now she saw it was good'. And three sentences later, it sets up the rapturous metaphor for unexpressed connubial delights: 'It was, for hours and hours, later on, as if she had somehow been lifted aloft, were floated and carried on some warm high tide beneath which stumbling-blocks had sunk out of sight.' Other examples: 'The conditions facing her had yielded, for the time, to the golden mist—had considerably melted away; but there they were again, definite, and it was for the next quarter of an hour as if she could have counted them one by one on her

Faulkner permits himself to evaluate under the guise of *as if*: 'On two pages one can find as many as fourteen evaluative comparisons, nine of them introduced with "as though" or "as if". This device may for some readers serve general realistic demands—it is "as if" the author really shared the human condition to the extent of not knowing for sure how to evaluate these events. But morally the effect is still a rigorous control over the reader's own range of judgments.' (p. 184) There is no need to suggest that Faulkner imitated James: clearly the utility of *as if* appeared independently to them (and to many other novelists) as a solution to a given esthetic problem.

As with other features, *The Portrait of a Lady* seems in advance of *The American* in respect to the use of 'as if' construction; it contains three in two hundred sentences, while *The American* contains none.

fingers'; '. . . the prime impression had remained, in the manner of a spying servant . . . It was as if he [the 'servant'] had found this pretext in her observed necessity of comparing—comparing the obvious common elements in her husband's and her stepmother's ways of now "taking" her'; 'They would then have been, all successfully, throwing dust in each other's eyes; and it would be at last as if they must turn away their faces, since the silver mist that protected them had begun to grow sensibly thin.'

That-clauses are often introduced by the expletive *it* and a verb; the verb is regularly other than the copula, indeed is often metaphoric: 'It did much for him . . . that the beginning of business awaited him'; '. . . it had broken on them all as a blessing that their absentee [Chad] *had* perhaps a conscience'; '. . . it wouldn't in the least help that [Milly] herself knew him, as quickly, for having been in her country and threshed it out'; in a mock-biblical mood, 'It came to pass before he moved that Waymarsh . . . struck him as the present alternative to the young man in the balcony'; '. . . it instantly stood out for [Maggie] that there was really no new judgment of them she should be able to show. . . .' *It* is essential if lively predicates of this sort are to be used with abstract propositions. The alternative is not possible: 'That Waymarsh struck him as the present alternative came to pass' is not English. Another frequent use of *it* is with verbs of hypothesis like *seem* and *appear*: '. . . it seemed a part of the swift prosperity of the American visitors that . . . [Kate] should yet appear so conscious . . . of possibilities of friendship for them'; 'It almost appeared to Milly that their fortune had been unduly precipitated'; '. . . it seemed to prove nothing, as against other things, that [Lord Mark] was bold . . .'

The construction with the infinitive also occurs, but to a lesser extent. Again James takes full advantage of the opportunity for imaginative predicates: 'It somehow ministered for him to indulgence to feel Waymarsh . . . as much tucked in as a patient in a hospital'; 'It upset him a little . . . to find himself at last remembering on what current of association he had been floated so far . . '; '. . . it immensely helped [Maggie] . . . to be able at

F

once to speak of the Prince as having done more to quicken than soothe her curiosity.' The passive also occurs, but to a lesser extent: 'it naturally couldn't have been known to [Strether] how much a spectator looking from one to the other might have discerned that they had in common'; and, with the reader as implicit subject, 'It will have sufficiently been seen that he was not a man to neglect any good chance for reflection.' The latter type, as a direct communication between narrator and reader is more common in the earlier 'omniscient' style; from *The American*: 'It is to be feared that [Newman's] perception of the difference between good architecture and bad was not acute . . .', 'To this it may be answered that he might have made another fortune, if he chose. . .'

12. EXPLETIVE *THERE*

There is, of course, another expletive particle in English, namely *there*. *There* is used chiefly to make minimal statements of existence: 'There is a car here' is equivalent to 'A car exists here'. The form ordinarily occurs with the indefinite article. With the definite article *there* is usually locative: 'There is the car' means 'The car is in that place'. The difference is pretty much that between French *il y a* and *voilà*.

Again James uses two or three times as many *theres* as do the other novelists. And again *The Portrait of a Lady* shows itself to be closer to the style of the later novels than to *The American*: there are fifteen main clauses beginning with *there* in the *Portrait* compared to only one in *The American*. Further, almost all of these anticipate abstract nouns. This would seem reasonable; it is the abstract noun whose existence must be asserted, since, unlike the character, it is not normally expected, in fiction, to be a topic. Naïve fiction usually requires *there* only to introduce a character the first time: 'There was a boy and his name was Tim', 'There once lived a couple in a forest', and so on.

Of nouns introduced by *there*, those of greatest interest to the present discussion are psychological. Peculiarly Jamesian are sentences which do not make explicit reference to a character in the main clause: 'There was little fear that they [Strether and Waymarsh] shouldn't see each other . . .' It is Strether, of course, who has so little fear about this 'sequel'; the irony is made more delicate by not bearing down on the mind in question. 'There was little doubt of the expression of face the sight of it [i.e. Strether's having Maria 'in a safe place'] would have produced in a certain person'; again the doubt is Strether's, but no need to specify that. 'There had been elements of impression in their half-hour over their watered beer-glasses that gave him his occasion for conveying that he held this compromise with his stiffer self to have become extreme'; not 'Strether had received impressions that . . .' nor 'Strether was impressed by . . .' but some disembodied elements of impression floating above beer-glasses. Or about Milly: 'There were more indications than she could reduce to order in the manner of the friendly niece'; or Maggie: '. . . she decided that if he should say nothing for another period of twenty-four hours she must take it as showing that they were, in her private phraseology, lost; so little possible sincerity could there be in pretending to care for a journey to Spain . . .' *There* may be used to set up an abstraction independent enough to take its own reflexive: 'Then . . . there had declared itself a readjustment of relations to which she was, once more, practically a little sacrificed': *there* attributes not only existence but autonomy to the abstraction.

Also very Jamesian is the use of *there* with deictic nouns; *anything*, *nothing*, and so on. Half the nouns with *there* in *The Wings of the Dove* passage are of this sort: '. . . was there anything but the senseless shifting tumble . . .?'; 'There would be nothing for her to explain or attenuate or brag about'; 'There were more things in this than the one that Lord Mark might have taken up'; '. . . there were things in that, probably, many things, as to which she would learn more . . .'; 'she didn't, none the less, otherwise protest against his remark; there was something else she was occupied in seeing'. This heavy use of *thing, nothing, something* in statements of bare existence is probably explained by the content of the chapter: Milly finds herself in a mystifying situation, full of undertones and currents that are beyond her. But she is clever and eager to learn, and so she asserts the existence of 'these things' and stores them away until she has time to identify them.

13. RELATIONS, ILLUSTRATIONS AND PLENITUDE

Mr. Watt has stressed the importance of 'multiplicity of relations' and the consequent multiplicity of vision in the Jamesian scheme:

. . . the defence of the Jamesian habit of mind must surely be that what the human vision shares with that of animals is presumably the perception of concrete images, not the power to conceive universals: such was Aristotle's notion of man's distinguishing capacity. The universals in the present context are presumably the awareness that behind every petty individual circumstance there ramifies an endless network of general, moral, social, and historical relations. Henry James' style can be seen as a supremely civilized effort to relate every event and every moment of life to the full complexity of circumambient conditions.[1]

The 'circumambient conditions' include personal relationships among the characters, and between them and their situation (the developed *donnée*). In a sense, of course, all fiction is concerned with relationships among characters and situations; what makes the later style of James special is the extent to which it struggles to *name* them, by ransacking grammar and lexicon and, beyond, the far realms of metaphor, and its exquisite ability to find, along the scale of generality, terms to fit the case. Even up to the most general terms of all, for James often has a character do no more

[1] Watt, p. 475.

than 'find a relation' in something, as if intensity could not but
inhere in relations, regardless of their nature.

What needs to be urged is that great emphasis is placed on the
palpability of these relations. I have already remarked the unusual
effect of giving thoughts, emotions, and a variety of other intangibles a life of their own, quite independent of the character
himself: Strether's 'conscience had been amusing itself, for the
forty-eight hours, by forbidding him purchase of a book'; after
Chad wrote 'that he had decided to go in for economy and the
real thing, Strether's fancy had quite fondly accompanied him in
this migration'; Maggie Verver 'never doubted of the force of
the feeling that bound her to her husband; but to become aware
almost suddenly that it had begun to vibrate with a violence
that had some of the effect of a strain would, rightly looked at,
after all, but show that she was, like thousands of women, every
day acting up to the full privilege of passion.' Symptomatic of the
autonomy of these 'things' is their use in reflexive constructions:
'She neglected his question for a little, partly because her attention
attached itself more and more to the handsome girl . . .'; 'whatever
it was it had showed in this brief interval as better than the
alternative; and it now presented itself altogether in the image and
in the place in which she had left it'.

Intangibility is deeply implicated in the whole Jamesian effect.
That effect is not an intense picture of physical reality, as, for
example, a Hemingway sought it—the way things really sound,
smell, feel. The physical environment is evoked only grudgingly
by James, as if out of a sense of duty, to flesh out the moral and
psychological problems that form the real substance. Environment is illustrative. Indeed everything is illustrative; and what is
illustrated is the matured seed, the *donnée*, which, as we learn so
clearly in the notebooks, is ever source and centre. Everything—
character, setting, atmosphere—is created to solve an esthetic
problem. James writes in his notebook that Howells' chance
remark to Sturges 'immediately . . . as everything, thank God,
does . . . suggests a little situation . . . it gives me the little idea of
the figure of an elderly man who hasn't "lived", hasn't at all, in

the sense of sensation, passions, impulses, pleasures—and to whom, in the presence of some great human spectacle, some great organization for the Immediate, the Agreeable, for curiosity, and experiment and perception, for Enjoyment, in a word, becomes *sur la fin*, or toward it, sorrowfully aware.'[1] The big abstractions are there at the outset, along with the 'elderly man', and they never disappear. Details are secondary,[2] chosen on grounds of plausibility or expedition: 'Say our friend is a widower . . . He may be an American—he might be an Englishman . . . It might be London, it might be Italy . . . He has been a great worker . . . But of what kind? I can't make him a novelist— too like W.D.H., and too generally *invraisemblable* . . . A clergyman is too obvious and *usé* . . . A journalist, a lawyer—these men WOULD in a manner have "lived" '. And on he goes in pursuit of the *vraisemblable*, the plausible. But it's all illustrative: he was not seized by a man, but by an abstract situation, and he is looking for a man to fit it, to make it likely.[3] Verisimilitude—not imitative realism—is the principle. '. . . All this must be—oh, so light, so delicately summarized, so merely touched. What I seem to see is the possibility of some little illustrative action.' 'Illustrative' is the keyword. The task is to find the flesh—and not too much of it, but enough—to adorn the situational skeleton. Is it difficult to understand then that the problem was as much How plentiful the details? as Which shall they be? To use the terms of Monroe Beardsley, James was as preoccupied by 'plenitude' as by 'congruence'—he wanted a sufficiency but no more, and he frequently admits how difficult it is to know how much detail to go into.

[1] Notebook entry for October 31, 1895, *The Notebooks of Henry James*, edited by F. O. Matthiessen and Kenneth B. Murdock (New York, 1961), p. 226.

[2] Cf. Percy Lubbock (*The Craft of Fiction*, New York, 1957, p. 160): Strether's 'grand adventure is not expressed in its incidents. These, as they are devised by the author, are secondary, they are the extensions of the moral event which takes place in the breast of the ambassador . . .'

[3] He wrote in 1901 to Howells: '. . . it had long before—it had in the very act of striking me as a germ—got away from you or from anything like you: had become impersonal and independent.'

There are frequent occasions in James' fiction when the narrator says he might have added more detail if he had had the time:

All sorts of other pleasant small things—small things that were yet large for [Strether]—flowered in the air of the occasion; but the bearing of the occasion itself on matters still remote concerns us too closely to permit us to multiply our illustrations. Two or three, however, in truth, we should perhaps regret to lose. The tortuous wall—girdle, long since mapped . . .

Or at another place, also early in *The Ambassadors*: 'All sorts of things in fact now seemed to come over him, comparatively few of which his chronicler can hope for space to mention'. He is like a lecturer who has twenty examples in his notes but lets himself decide on the podium how many to use so that he will end precisely on the hour. The Jamesian equivalent of 'ending on the hour' is to pace the novel so that the high point of the action comes neither too late nor too soon; illustrative detail is adjusted to that requirement, following the principle of 'foreshortening'. And since he was an economical writer it is not incomprehensible that James should have preferred to achieve plenitude through single high order abstractions rather than through assemblages of concrete particulars, to write 'phenomena' rather than 'chatter, candlelight, plates, silver, jewelry', and so on. The abstraction in James' hands is open-ended, an impressionistic device evoking all that and much more.

But a consequence is that the style moves away from, not toward, drama. For acts become nominalized, and their predicate is the copula, the verb form for exposition, for a listing of particulars and propositions. Instead of actors performing on a stage, there are increasing numbers of statements of the existence of things. What action there is tends to be durative, not momentaneous; one state of affairs prevails until replaced by another. Usually the very noun is durative: 'understanding', 'enjoyment', 'relation', 'sense', 'detachment'—nouns of continuous behaviour. Similarly, there are many plurals without definite articles. They are *examplary*: they summarize rather than dramatize the behaviour of the characters. They occur often in series, to the same

effect as the large abstractions, giving an impression of the full
life but without the details: 'These were fine facilities, pleasantries,
ironies, all these luxuries of gossip and philosophies of London
and of life, and they became quickly, between the pair, the common form of talk'; '. . . There were moreover the other facets of the
selection and decision that this demonstration of her own had
required . . .' James' fondness for this effect is clearly evident
in the revision of *Roderick Hudson*. Where the original describes
Mary as 'a woman for whom he himself [Rowland] had been
keeping in reserve for years a deeply characteristic passion', the
revised version has 'a woman at whose disposition he himself had
been keeping, from the moment of his first meeting her, a secret
fund of strange alacrities'. Similarly, in the original, Roderick
'had a wonderfully proper accent [in Italian], though in reading
aloud he ruined the sense of half the lines he rolled off so sonor-
ously'; in the revision, 'he ruined half his admirations and
felicities'. Another example: Rowland, 'in the geniality of a mood
attuned to the mellow charm of a Roman villa . . .' becomes
attuned rather, in the later version, 'to all the stored patiences that
lurk in Roman survivals'. And '. . . this mere passive enjoyment of
grandeur' becomes '. . . this mere passive enjoyment of grandeur,
and . . . this perpetual platitude of spirit under imposed admirations.'

Abstraction in the service of plenitude entails a form of semantic
ellipsis. It is less that the things James' characters do are interesting
in themselves than that they are 'representative'. Scene may have
been important to James in theory, but in practice conditions and
relations and actions are very frequently introduced in a most
directly enunciated, totally unscenic, way. That is why observa-
tions by Percy Lubbock, like the following about James' com-
mitment to 'drama', though very precious as insights into the
novelty of his method, are somewhat overstated: 'The world of
silent thought is thrown open, and instead of telling the reader
what happened there, the novelist uses the look and behavior
of thought as the vehicle by which the story is rendered.'[1] It is

---

[1] Lubbock, p. 157.

a little difficult to follow this, because Lubbock provides few examples to illuminate his metaphors: what, for instance, *is* 'the look and behavior of thought'? The fact is that James usually does *tell* us what happened in the world of silent thought, does so in so many words by naming (assigning a noun to) the mental act: 'His idea was to begin business immediately . . .'; '. . . there were more things in his mind than so few days could account for . . .'; 'her sensibility was almost too sharp for her comfort'; 'there would be nothing for her to explain or attenuate or brag about'; 'This consciousness of its having answered with her husband was the uplifting, sustaining wave'; and so on. Even in a metaphoric sense it is hard to see how this could be called 'dramatic'. When James writes of Maggie that 'The conditions facing her had yielded, for the time, to the golden mist . . .' there may be a scene evoked but hardly one that could appear on any stage. Only in the extreme cases, when the mental operations are actually personified, become characters, do we seem to get a genuine sense of 'drama'. Most of the sentences describing the inner life, even when they are lively, are not dramatic in this way. There's a lot of vigorous thinking going on, to be sure, but it doesn't seem particularly helpful to call it 'dramatic':

Everything he wanted was comprised moreover in a single boon— the common, unattainable art of taking things as they came. He appeared to himself to have given his best years to an active appreciation of the way they didn't come; but perhaps—as they would seemingly here be things quite other—this long ache might at last drop to rest. He could easily see that from the moment he should accept the notion of his foredoomed collapse the last thing he would lack would be reasons and memories. Oh, if he *should* do the sum, no slate would hold the figures!

Much of *The Ambassadors* is in this mode—the reminiscence may be Strether's but the statement of it is more or less expository. The narrator *tells* us, he summarizes years of Strether's history, he interprets whole realms of behaviour in a word: 'boon', 'art', 'appreciation'. Even the metaphor of the slate is interpretive— we are not witnessing 'the look and behavior of thought', but its end product, its conclusion. After Joyce and other stream-of-consciousness writers, can it be seriously maintained that this is the very *process* of thought?[1]

But what Lubbock says certainly has its element of truth; we do sense something in James that fits his description, that '. . . instead of a man upon the stage, concealing and betraying his thought, we watch the thought itself, the hidden thing, as it twists to and fro in his brain—watch it without any other aid to understanding but such as its own manner of bearing my supply . . . The novelist . . . could step forward and explain the restless appearance of the man's thought. But if he prefers the dramatic way, admittedly the more effective, there is nothing to prevent him from taking it. The man's thought, in its turn, can be made to reveal its own inwardness.'[2] Though the thought often is not hidden but directly expressed or interpreted by a narrator, it is true that the interpretation is usually light-handed: we have already mentioned the frequency of sentences in which James felt it sufficient to say simply that a character had 'an association' or 'a reaction' or whatever. It seems to be a matter of degree; James' narrator often interprets, indeed usually interprets, but he is very subtle about it and *seems* not to intrude. He is very careful not to interpret too much, not to tell us, for example, *why* such and such a thought occurs to Strether at that moment, or why he thinks about it in the way that he does or what its deeper significance might be—for example, there is no hint that his sense of

---

[1] There are several instances of a removal from Strether's point of view, when the narrator assumes a completely privileged vantage. For example, in the first chapter he describes Maria on the basis of a knowledge of her personality and prior history which Strether could not yet possess: Maria 'was in truth, it may be communicated, the mistress of a hundred cases or categories, receptacles of the mind, subdivisions for inconvenience, in which, from a full experience, she pigeon-holed her fellow mortals with a hand as free as that of a compositor scattering type.' See Booth, pp. 42–50, for a general discussion of the flexibility of James' practice compared to the rigidity of his followers in fictional theory. And see also his excellent discussion of the misleadingness of the term 'dramatic', pp. 161–3.

[2] Lubbock, pp. 157–8.

loss of wife and son is mixed up with his general sense of lost opportunity, chances missed, and so on. That general kind of interpretation is never made. As Lubbock puts it, James never 'expounds' the substance of Strether's thought; he is content to give us its mere surface. And an important way to insure that it is only surface is to keep the thoughts vague, incipient, inchoate, yet to be formed: 'Nothing could have been more odd than Strether's feeling, at that moment, that he was launched in something of which the sense would be quite disconnected from the sense of his past, and which was literally beginning there and then.' Vague portents loom up—*that* is the surface of Strether's mind.

14. ELEGANT VARIATION

How does intangibility work together with other devices—elegant variation, hyperbole, ellipsis, colloquial diction, and metaphor—to achieve the distinctively Jamesian texture?

Elegant variation is by no means limited to characters—James names things and abstractions in this manner too. The stylistic motive for synonymic variation may seem the logical opposite of that of repetition of pronouns when the sense would be clearer by the use of a noun. But the rhetorical effect is similar: both are ways of pre-selecting the audience. In the act of following the various changes in appellation, in seeing the unity among the terms, the reader cannot avoid an analytical stance. To go back again to the first paragraph of *The Ambassadors*: Strether has a 'secret principle' which operates and is instinctive—a 'fruit' of a 'sharp sense' of something. The principle is then referred to more vaguely as an 'everything' (mixed with it is an 'apprehension'). Finally it is a 'happier device'. It takes time and effort to recognize that each of these names essentially the same thing, and to ask why the variety is necessary, why, for example, a 'principle' should be a 'fruit' and then a 'device', why that device should be 'happier' than some other device, and what that other device might be. The effort involved—like the effort to identify pronouns—is, presumably, salubrious: it promotes a thoughtful, a puzzling-out-attitude, the kind of reading that James wanted.

15. ELLIPSIS

Something similar may be said about the relation between intangibility and ellipsis. The combination of the two is perhaps James' most characteristic effect, an effect making heavy demands upon the reader's patience and counting upon his appreciation of the allusive and the vaguely rich. Consider, for example, Susan Stringham's 'princess' metaphor in *The Wings of the Dove*: princesses, she remarks, live 'on the plane of mere elegant representation. That was why they pounced, at city gates, on deputed flower-strewing damsels' (like Kate). 'Representation' is difficult not only because it is abstract but because its syntactic completion is left to the reader: representation of whom or what? Or of whom or what *as* whom or what? Do princesses represent themselves as merely elegant? Or merely represent themselves as elegant? Or elegantly represent themselves as themselves? Or something or someone else? Or is it their 'realm' that they represent (or represent as something)? Or is it elegance in the abstract that they represent? The possibilities seem to dwindle off into a hazy 'rich' distance. Or from *The Golden Bowl*: 'The dazzling person [Amerigo] was upstairs and she was down, and there were moreover the other facts of the selection and decision that this demonstration of her own had required . . .' But what in fact had Maggie selected and decided? Again, because the terms are opened to speculation, the sense of their intangibility is magnified.

Ellipsis with abstractions seems the natural order for James; indeed, completion, when it comes, sometimes sounds like an afterthought: recall the elaborate metaphor from *The Golden Bowl* discussed above (p. 75), in which an 'impression' becomes a 'spying servant': 'It was as if he [the servant] had found this pretext in her observed necessity of comparing—comparing the obvious common elements in her husband's and her stepmother's ways of now "taking" her.' The repetition and completion of 'comparing' suggest some kind of last-minute, grudging concession to the reader, who is struggling to understand (among other things) the oblique phrase 'in her observed necessity' (Jamesian for something like 'in observing the sense of necessity she felt'). But the direct object that is supplied—with its 'elements' and its finicky special sense of ' "taking" '—raises as many questions as it answers. Thus, the rectification is a 'pseudo-rectification' (to use an expression of Dwight Macdonald's); it occurs at the cost of the need for a new rectification.

In the narrower sense, ellipsis refers to the actual deletion of words normally required by the grammar, so that the construction is technically incomplete; the words and structures must be inferred from the context. But the term may also be used in a broader sense, to refer to the withholding of any kind of information that would help explain things, though the sentence in question may be technically complete as far as syntax goes. It is particularly this latter kind that is very widespread in James' later style.

Even in simpler cases, ellipsis exacts additional effort from the reader, and when it is extreme or extended (as not infrequently in James' later style), considerable energy may be required of the reader, an expenditure that might seem unrequited to anyone who insists on conclusive results. It is characteristic of the knottiness of the style that ellipsis, either alone or together with other complicating elements, often leaves even the diligent reader in doubt as to what precisely has been said. Extensive ellipsis cannot but breed ambiguity, and in James' case it is ambiguity of a vaguer rather than a sharper kind.

Perhaps the best way to demonstrate this is to show how uncertainties accumulate in a passage of even moderate length.

The reader must understand that this demonstration is not meant as a critique. When discussing matters like ellipsis, ambiguity, and vagueness, it is difficult not to give the impression that the thing should be cleared up in some way. However, that is not my intention, and if the reader assumes it to be, it is because I am a victim of the limitations of our current critical language. I am not interested in 'correcting' James, but rather in demonstrating, as precisely as I can, the points at which reading him becomes difficult. That does not mean that I condemn the difficulties; on the contrary, I believe them to be justifiable in terms of the larger effects that he seeks. Fellow-admirers of the later style will, I think, understand my intentions; those who dislike that style will use the analysis precisely to attack James; but then they can use this whole account for that purpose. If one believes categorically that abstractness, vagueness, ellipsis, and so on are bad *in themselves*, then, of course, James' later style must seem a failure.

My example is from James' non-fiction, where the effect is exaggerated because there is no context of plot or character to help the reader along. Consider the first several sentences of the Preface to the New York edition of *The Aspern Papers*:

(1) I not only recover with ease, but I delight to recall, the first impulse given to the idea of 'The Aspern Papers'.

The beginning is fairly simple, although we never do feel completely certain about the origin of the 'impulse' because of ellipsis of the agent of the past participle, that is, the subject of the underlying transformed sentence of which the participle was predicate. 'X gave the first impulse'. What could X be? James' experiences in Italy? A specific incident? General circumstances? He himself? We are given at the outset two unexplained terms: 'impulse' and the subject of 'gave', and these are the first of several irresolutions which we must abide.

The second sentence is much more difficult.

(2) It is at the same time true that my present mention of it may perhaps too effectually dispose of any complacent claim to my having 'found' the situation.

Though the sentence is not lengthy, it raises so many questions that even the diligent reader is likely to be stopped in his tracks.

At the same time . . .: The sentence adverb plays a disjunctive role—it seems to mean about the same thing as 'yet'. But the antithesis between the second and the first sentence does not emerge clearly, because the members are in different logical sets. 'I easily recover and delightfully recall the impulse; yet . . .' An antithesis requires partial parallelism to make its contrast pointed; in this case it *could* have been one of grammatical subject—'Yet *my reader* might not feel that ease and delight' (antithesis of 'I'). Or of predicate—'yet I despair of *communicating* that ease and delight' (antithesis of 'recall'). But neither, of course, is meant; the antithesis is muffled—we get as the opposing member 'my present mention of it' (which internally raises its own difficulties, as we shall see in a moment). And the second predicate, 'dispose of', does not parallel 'recover' and 'recall'; whatever James may be understood to be doing in the second sentence, it is not an action which is *obviously* in the same universe of discourse as that of the first. The reader cannot but feel the ground shift; and 'at the same time' not only does not help but seems actually to hinder. In other words, it is not in the least clear (as 'at the same time' suggests it is) how 'easily and delightfully recalling a creative impulse' should lead logically to 'disposing of claims to having "found" it' (whatever the special sense of 'found' may turn out to be).

. . . *my present mention*: Does 'mention' mean *mere* mention, that is, 'only touching on the topic' (note that the transitory sense would be heightened by the gerundive form); or does it mean, by litotes, 'this preface, this whole ten-page discussion'? Impossible to be sure, though how 'merely' mentioning a situation could dispose of the claim that it had been 'found' is rather difficult to imagine. Neither alternative, of course, involves ellipsis in the strict sense, but at the same time neither is totally unrelated to it since a fuller treatment would have resolved the question ('my present mention, which is all this preface pretends to be', or the like). If, further, 'only touching upon' is meant, then there is an additional ambiguity implicit in the degree of emphasis to be placed on 'present'—does it mean *simply* 'mentioning it', or mentioning it *now* (as opposed to mentioning it at some other time—'the fact that I mention it now rather than another time is what disposes of any claim, etc. . . .')?

. . . *of it*: The old pronoun reference problem—of what? The impulse? The idea? *The Aspern Papers*? The situation? And if the second or fourth, are these the same ('elegant variants') or separate, in other words is it 'the idea' *or* 'the situation' or 'the idea, *i.e.*, the situation'? Unidentified pronouns entail a kind of ellipsis in the sense that something is omitted, namely the referent itself, which could have been used instead.

. . . *may perhaps* . . . *dispose of* . . .: It is not the otioseness of 'may perhaps' that is troublesome, but the very introduction of elements of possibility without clear motivation; this is clearly elliptical in the broader sense of the word. Is it that 'the present mention' may *seem* to dispose of the claim, but that in fact it does not ('may' of appearance)? Or that it does in fact dispose of it, and the author is sorry for that ('may' of admission)? Or that he does indeed wish to dispose of the claim, but he does not want to appear to do it in too dissembling a way; that is, he is going to give the reader a chance to follow the line of reasoning and reach a conclusion of his own ('may' of concession)? Or something else? We are never told; the ground shifts again in the next sentence, as we shall see, to the question of what ' "find" ' shall be taken to mean.

. . . *too effectually* . . .: Both words are ambiguous, the latter semantically, the former by ellipsis of the correlative element. 'Effectually', *Webster's Third* tells us, can mean either 'with great effort' or 'effectively, decisively' (leaving out more obviously inappropriate senses like 'actually' and the obsolete 'earnestly'). The intensifier 'too' calls desperately for its other half—'too effectually to do what?'—but we are left again in the world of the inferential. Too effectually to be convincing? To permit any deeper inquiry, say into the nature of ' "finding" '? To reflect the insight into his own creative process that an author can reasonably hope to have? Or something else? This is the crucial word in the sentence—everything else turns on it, but it remains tantalizingly unclear.

   . . . any complacent claim to my having 'found' the situation. . . . :
'Any complacent claim' is an elliptical nominalization of a predicate whose underlying subject is deleted. Is it a claim made or makeable by the author, or by someone or something else? The appearance of 'my' two words later, the fact that the claim is 'complacent', and the principle of simplicity suggest the former, but the phrase still needs to be puzzled out. The quotation marks around ' "found" ' are probably, as often in James, allusive, to show that the word has here a bigger or more special sense than usually. What that sense is can only be divined from the context, and sometimes not even then; questions continue to reverberate about what special meaning may be intended. Some effort is made in this instance to specify the sense, however, as we shall see. 'Situation' has already been discussed in connection with 'it', but it is important to bear in mind the uncertainty of whether it is or is not completely synonymous with 'idea' in sentence one.

These then are the problems of sentence two. But merely listing them does not give an adequate picture of the *degree* of uncertainty that the reader faces. For the uncertainty is not simply the sum of the alternatives but their *product*; the ambiguity is not arithmetical but geometric, exponential. They do not merely combine, they multiply. When there are three sets of events and each allows two alternatives, the total number of alternatives is not six $(2 + 2 + 2)$ but eight $(2 \times 2 \times 2)$. Assuming that the above discussion of this sentence reasonably represents the ambiguities and that my calculations are correct, there are, theoretically, 960 readings of this sentence $(2 \times 5 \times 4 \times 4 \times 3 \times 2)$! Even if we eliminate the final ambiguity, deciding that the 'claim' can only be the author's—the possibilities number 480. But, of course, these 960 (or 480) readings are not equally likely, nor do most of the differences amount to very much in terms of the general sense of the whole essay. Still, there is enough uncertainty to lead to a feeling of uneasiness, especially if one pursues the matter too

G

relentlessly. But that, of course, is the wrong spirit. It is not that the reader is ever totally confused or that the ambiguities amount to logical contradictions, but that certain vague questions are raised which can never be completely resolved. It is as if James expects his reader to half-know what he means before he says it. A certain degree of the uncertainty may be cleared up in the broader context but never all of it. For example, most of the questions posed by the second sentence are not answered by the third and fourth, which go off on another tangent, raising their own problems:

(3) Not that I quite know indeed what situations the seeking fabulist does 'find'; he seeks them enough assuredly, but his discoveries are, like those of the navigator, the chemist, the biologist, scarce more than alert recognitions.

(4) He *comes upon* the interesting thing as Columbus came upon the isle of San Salvador, because he had moved in the right direction for it— also because he knew, with the encounter, what 'making land' then and there represented.

Not that piles one concession on another, further sidetracking the reader, who has not yet figured out the basis of the first ('at the same time'), though the latter seems more straightforward, turning on the meaning of a word explicitly occurring in the text, namely 'find'. But the expression is odd and oblique: the sense must be 'whether the seeking fabulist does in fact "find situations"', this much seems clear from the part after the semicolon—'he seeks them enough . . . but his discoveries are . . . scarce more than alert recognitions'. But the emphasis is twisted from 'whether' to 'what' (that is, 'which'). Again the difficulty arises from ellipsis—what is to be inferred is not 'which situations among all those presented to him' but rather 'which situations *if there are any* . . .' It is precisely the explanatory element which remains unspecified, left to the reader's inference, and the context forces a radical revision of first assumptions.

'Indeed' is a sentence adverb (made more difficult by omission of commas and shift of position—'Indeed, not that I quite know', or 'Not that I quite know, indeed', would have been clearer).

But it is not so certain that 'assuredly' is, though it probably is; the sense is doubtless 'Assuredly, he seeks them enough' rather than 'He seeks them enough in an assured manner' (and certainly not 'He seeks them in an assured enough manner'), but again there is a moment's hesitation. As for 'quite', is it that James is not sure that he knows? Or that his knowledge is not accurate, although he knows to some degree? Or something else? He must know *something*, since how else could he go on to make the distinction between mere 'finding' and 'alert recognitions'? In other words, is the expression merely a bit of false modesty, or should it be taken more seriously? Ellipsis of the object of 'discoveries' and 'recognitions' is not so troublesome, because it is implicit in 'them', referring back to 'situations', which is object of 'seeks'. The basic antithesis is, fairly clearly, between ' "finds" ' and '(alertly) recognizes', if the context of sentence four, and particularly the clause 'because he moved in the right direction for it', is assigned the importance it seems to demand. The difference entails elements of surprise, unexpectedness, unlikelihood: ' "find" ' in this context seems to mean 'stumble upon by chance', as opposed to 'alert recognition' which is the proper reward of the man who knows what he is looking for, who, because he is experienced and has sought long and hard, is *prepared* to make a discovery. He recognizes the good thing because he has spent years sifting among good and bad things; only the novice ' "finds" ', that is, hits upon the good thing by accident. 'Discoveries' is a prop, a noun deixis, to hold the subject in focus so that James can tell us what the fabulist *does* do, since he does not 'find' his situations; therefore, it does not enter into the antithesis between ' "find" ' and 'recognize', but mediates between them.

These discriminations have not come easily; they cost James a pair of quotation marks and the extra adjective 'alert' (remember how he disapproved of adjectives). The struggle is underlined by the italics of *'comes upon'* (which reminds me, unfairly, of an Italian lady who reacted to my ignorance of a word she used by saying it more loudly). The italics serve the same function as do the quotation marks around ' "find" '; they inform the reader that the meaning is more special than it might seem, more special than that of the neutral or normative 'discovers', that 'comes upon' is in the class of 'recognitions', which has come to mean— by contrast with mere 'finding'—discovery as the result of *experienced* searching or the like. But this is no ordinary sense of 'come upon', and the reader feels the strain.

The chief problem in sentence four, of course, is the simile, which is complex enough to require a table:

VEHICLE	TENOR
1. 'Columbus'	1. The author
2. *'comes upon'* (see above)	2. 'comes upon' (see above)
3. 'San Salvador'	3. 'the interesting thing'
4. physically 'moved in the right direction for it'. i.e., by his expert use of compass, stars, theory of geography, etc. . . .	4. mentally moved in the right direction for it, i.e., by his previous experience as a novelist in distinguishing between promising and unpromising leads.
5. 'he knew . . . what "making land" then and there represented', i.e., that it must be the New World, since other geographical areas would not occur at that longitude and latitude.	5. [This is the difficult part: see below.]
6. 'Nature had so placed it' (land).	6. 'history, "literal history" . . . had . . . thrown off a curious flower' (that is, this functions as the vehicle of *another* metaphor).

The simile goes along smoothly enough until we get to the fifth part. First of all, it is a bit unsettling to have quotation marks around 'making land'; they cannot mean that the phrase is only figurative, since Columbus did in fact make land. Possibly they are meant to show that the expression is slang or technical or the like. More importantly, what is the precise counterpart of 'making land' for the novelist? Is it simply reaching the decision that a given situation is in fact worth recounting, that it does provide the proper size grist for one's mill? Probably so, though one wonders if there might not be some reference to a certain *part* of the process, since presumably Columbus saw the island from a distance before he 'made' it. Again a bit of uncertainty. James had the opportunity of spelling things out in a balder, less elliptical way, by identifying the reference of *what*—'he knew that "making land" then and there meant that he had discovered the New World'—but he preferred to leave it to the reader to infer that conclusion (if that is the proper conclusion).

With the encounter is also an elliptical alternative to some more straightforward expression, perhaps a clause like 'When he encountered land': the verb is nominalized and connected with the peculiar 'with' ('at the encounter' would seem less so), and both subject and object are deleted. There is little ambiguity, however.

(5) Nature had so placed it, to profit—if as profit we may measure the matter!—by his fine unrest, just as history, 'literary history' we in this connexion call it, had in an out-of-the-way corner of the great garden of life thrown off a curious flower that I was to feel worth gathering as soon as I saw it.

'So' is another stumbling-block. Is it a place-time adverb or pro-adverb, meaning 'then and there', 'at that time and in that place?' Then it would be a (not untypically Jamesian) inversion, for 'Nature had placed it so' (in which case 'to profit' is elliptical for 'in order to', or 'in order for it or for him to'). Or is it correlative with 'to', with ellipsis of an intervening 'as', namely 'Nature had placed it so as to profit . . . by his fine unrest?' The comma after 'it' is presumably there to help us, but it does not solve the problem. Our decision is complicated by two other factors:

(1) the need to identify the referent of 'it'. 'Land' seems most likely, rather than 'encounter' since the latter, an action, would not go very well with the tenor, 'the curious flower';

(2) the elliptical 'to profit' and the apologetic qualification 'if as profit we may measure the matter!' To whose profit? And why the uncertainty? Is the profit Columbus's? Certainly it was to his profit, and to the profit of the Spanish monarchy, and to the profit of the whole of Europe, that the New World was discovered. Yet it seems difficult to assume that the beneficiary is one of these human agents, since the syntax is more comfortably construed if 'Nature' or 'it' is the implicit subject of the verb 'profit'—either 'Nature had placed the island so that (or "so, in order that") Nature would profit . . .' or 'Nature had placed the island so that (or "so, in order that") the island would profit. . . .' Not much difference since the island is clearly a part of Nature; but there are hints of local benefits lurking in the second that are absent from the first. In either case, however, the apologetic interpolation 'if as profit we may measure the matter' would seem to refer to the *oddness* of speaking of 'profit' in reference to non-human things, Nature, or that hunk of land in particular. Or is there some other implication, of a Rousseauesque cast, that neither Nature in general nor San Salvador in particular stood to profit by man's despoliation? Or is it, on the contrary, that the discovery was *so* valuable and important historically that the word 'profit' cannot do justice to its significance? How does one decide?

'Fine' entails a more comfortable ambiguity: it is 'enriching', in the Empsonian sense, to think of Columbus' *unrest* as being at once 'excellent', 'exquisite', 'exact', 'subtle', and so on.

The problems in the tenor are no less considerable. Note first of all that setting 'Nature' in opposition to 'history', making the former ahistorical, is hardly a usual order. The two principles, diachrony and synchrony, are first opposed on an equal footing, but the former is immediately narrowed down to a special subclass, 'literary history'. However, both the context and the italics (which one now reacts to with a nervous tic) prompt us to avoid too early an identification with the profession of Taine and Saintsbury. 'History, "literary history"; we in this connexion call it' is Jamesian word order for 'History which we call, in this connexion, "literary history" ' or the like; it is not the syntax which is troublesome, but the sense in which the phrase ' "literary" ' is intended. (The quotation-marks must simply mean citation or definition of an expression *as* an expression.) One sense would suggest an immodesty: it was the history of English literature that (to its own profit) found the subject for James because anything he should do would surely find a place in its annals. But that assumption seems disproved by the explanation of the 'curious flower'; we are told two pages later that Jane Clairmond, the half-sister of Mary Godwin, mistress to Byron and mother of his daughter Allegra, had lived in Florence until late into the nineteenth century.

Thus, the rest of the simile might be indicated as follows:

VEHICLE OF FIRST SIMILE	TENOR OF FIRST = SIMILE	VEHICLE OF SECOND SIMILE	TENOR OF SECOND SIMILE
6. 'Nature had so placed'	6. 'history, "literary history" . . . had . . . thrown off'	6. (a personification expressing the fact that James had discovered the late existence in Florence of Jane Clairmond)	
7. 'it'	7. 'a curious flower'	7. the fact of Jane Clairmond's existence	
	8. 'in an out-of-the-way corner of the great garden of life'	8. X	

What is X? The glorious city of Florence is hardly an out-of-the-way corner. Perhaps the reference is to Jane Clairmond's home in a more restricted sense—to the fact, perhaps, that even in Florence few people knew of her existence. Even more likely it is not a literal reference to her whereabouts at all, 'out-of-the-way' being equivalent to 'out of history', that is, simply 'unknown'.

The next two sentences are clear enough:

(6) I got wind of my positive fact, I followed the scent.

(7) It was in Florence years ago; which is precisely, of the whole matter, what I like most to remember.

The simile is continued in 'got wind off' and 'followed the scent', whose tenors are obvious. It is useful at this point to collect ourselves, and to list all the terms, all the elegant variants which have been used to refer to what was first called 'idea' in the first sentence: 'idea' (1), 'it' (2), 'situation' (3), 'the interesting thing' (4), 'a curious flower' (5), 'my positive fact' (why 'positive'?). 'The scent' (6) is probably not the idea itself but certain hints of the idea. 'The whole matter' sounds like not only the idea but the entire process of composition, the idea plus James' reaction to it, his early sketches, in short, everything having to do with *The Aspern Papers*. Elegant variation, a kind of super-specification, may seem to be precisely the opposite of ellipsis, but we have seen that it makes similar demands on the reader, particularly—as often in James—when the equivalences are not clear. Then the reader finds himself wondering whether Y really *is* X or whether a new substance has been introduced.

(8) The air of the old-time Italy invests it, a mixture that on the faintest invitation I rejoice again to inhale—and this in spite of the mere cold renewal, ever, of the infirm side of that felicity, the sense, in the whole element, of things too numerous, too deep, too obscure, too strange, or even simply too beautiful, for any ease of intellectual relation.

Does 'it' refer to 'the whole matter' or more narrowly to the 'positive fact, the situation'? The metaphor of inhaling stands for recalling the atmosphere of 'the old-time Italy', so that 'this' must represent the whole process of reminiscing; it is elliptical for 'I rejoice to do this', or the like. The going gets more difficult immediately thereafter.

'In spite of' what? 'The mere cold renewal . . . of the infirm side of that [note: not 'my' or even 'one's'] felicity'? 'That felicity' is presumably the pleasure of his reminiscence, since merely *being* in Italy would not necessarily entail infirmities; but what is its 'infirm side'? Probably what is spelled out in the apposition, the sense of things too numerous, etc., to relate. But why 'infirm'?

Why should 'things' that are deep, even 'beautiful', have an 'infirm side'? Is it that not 'they' but rather 'he' has an infirm side? If so, this is another instance where ellipsis of personal reference makes the locution difficult. 'My felicity had an infirm side' would mean something like 'my happiness in recalling the old-time Italy, and so on, in spite of the fact that I knew (or know) that I could not capture all of it, because it was too manifold, deep, obscure, etc. . . .' It was beyond his power; he was too infirm, too weak, too incompetent to do it.

Ellipsis of personal reference continues throughout the sentence: not 'my sense' but 'the sense'. The formality of neutral deixis is purchased at the expense of clarity. The same process is repeated at the end of the sentence: again the verb is nominalized and the subject and object deleted—not 'for me to feel intellectually easy about', or 'to permit me [or 'one' or 'the author'] to relate it [the element, the situation] easily', or even 'for *my* intellectual ease . . .': but 'for *any* ease of intellectual relation'. The insistence on an elliptical manner introduces in 'intellectual' an additional difficulty: the word is perhaps introduced to help obviate the ambiguity of 'relation' alone, which can mean not only 'telling' but also 'relationship' or the like (is it 'relation of X' or 'relation to X'?). Yet it doesn't resolve that question at all, and indeed sets up little eddies of its own ('intellectual' as opposed to 'emotional'? or what?). The basic problem is the nominalization, and no mere adjectival ornament that does not include reference to implicit subject and/or object is going to make the reader's task simpler. On the contrary.

Going back a bit, we also wonder why the 'renewal' is a 'mere' renewal. ('Cold' seems more obvious; it is cold presumably because it throws a damper on the reminiscence, the 'warm' memory.) Is it 'mere' because he has learned, philosophically, to pay attention to such recognitions of his inadequacy? Or that once something is done, it's done, and there's no point in crying over spilt milk? Or that it is nothing *more* than a renewal, that is, he recognizes that he has already accepted his 'infirmity' and needn't but make passing reference to it? Or what? And the same thing might be said of 'ever'—does this happen every time he recalls this particular effort? Or Italy in general? Or the impossibility of recapturing the full complexity, depth, obscurity of *any* situation?

It is best to stop here, to leave it to the reader to pursue the vague beauties of the elliptical style of this Preface. I must repeat that my intention is not critical, though unhappily I find it hard to express myself except in traditional terms, with their normative implications. I admire James' ability to make us feel the vagueness of the inchoate creative state. I think the form suits the content and would have it no other. What I have tried to do is to locate as precisely as I can the sources of that vagueness and allusiveness; my wish is to demonstrate that a good part of it derives from ellipsis, particularly as the result of the reduction of clauses by nominalization of the predicate and deletion of the underlying subject and/or object. A great deal of the effect of vagueness and uncertainty would disappear if those clauses had been kept intact.

Of course, our chief interest in the penchant for ellipsis in James' style is esthetic; that is, we wonder about its functions in the total effect of his fiction. One of these surely is the 'screening' among readers that we have already noted in reference to the problem of pronoun identification; clearly the lazy reader will be turned off by the constant need to complete phrases and sentences and may resent the implication that he 'has to write part of the novel himself'. Another, I think, is the heavy sense of *portent* noted by Watt and other critics. Surely the best illustrations come from that most portentous of short stories, *The Beast in the Jungle*.

So, while they grew older together, she did watch^with him, and so she let this association^give shape and colour to her own existence. Beneath *her* forms^as well^detachment^had learned to sit and^behaviour had become for her, in the social sense^, a false account of herself.^ There was but one account^of her^that would have been true all the while, and that^she could give, directly^, to nobody, least of all to John Marcher. Her whole attitude^was a virtual statement^, but the perception of that^only seemed destined to take its place for him as one of the many things necessarily crowded out of his consciousness. If she had, moreover, like himself, to make sacrifices to their real truth^, it was to be granted that her compensation^might have affected her as more prompt and more natural.

I have marked with carets the places where further information would be at least helpful, if not actually essential. 'Watch' of course is intransitive, in the sense of 'keep vigil', but still a prepositional object is implied, something like 'for the remarkable thing that is to happen to Marcher'. It is precisely stylistic, I think, that the 'the remarkable thing, the spring of the beast out of the jungle' has become so omnipresent, so dominant in the action, that reference to it is unnecessary, that it is highlighted precisely by being elided. Here is a syntactic absence which calls attention to a psychological presence, Marcher's sense of imminent doom; James has made something functionally important out of nothing. Similarly, 'this association' is more pregnant than 'the association that she had with him' or the like; 'this' is not a mere equivalent of 'her', for it is not simply that she is associated with him, but that she is associated with him in this fearsome matter, this spooky 'watching'. The reader's pace is arrested by the word because its more expected sense would be 'mental connection, or relating things together'. The absence of a context suited to that meaning makes us switch to the other.

The next sentence also contains ellipses. Is the sense 'Beneath her forms of social behavior, or the like, as well as beneath his, detachment had learned to sit'? Or is 'her forms' being contrasted with something else of hers, say her 'substance'. Or is 'as well' equivalent to 'also' in the sense of 'additionally to their watching and to her permitting the association to give shape and colour to her own existence'? The first interpretation is correct, since in the previous paragraph, over a hundred words back, there occurs the statement that 'She was in the secret of the difference between the forms he went through—those of his little office under Government, those of caring for his modest patrimony, for his library, for his garden in the country, for the people in London whose invitations he accepted and repaid—and the detachment that reigned beneath them and that made of all behavior, all that could in the least be called behavior, a long act of dissimulation.' James expects us to remember 'forms', 'detachment', and 'reigned' at that distance, and to interpret the odd preposition 'beneath'. But sovereigns reign above, not beneath. Perhaps detachment is seen as sitting and reigning 'beneath' as a clown's sadness 'sits beneath' his comic task (the mask in fact is used metaphorically in an intervening sentence). James, typically, makes what is really complicated more so by leaving out words and taxing our memory, and by 'compensating' for the omission by extra highlighting on what is there, that is by putting 'her' in italics.

In the next clause, we are first confronted with the ambiguity of 'for her'—is it internal, i.e., 'in her view', or external, 'to look at her' or 'as far as one could tell'? The former seems more likely in view of the fact that it is the reflexive 'herself' that is used rather than 'her'. Note, too, how the word 'behavior' in the context of the whole sentence takes on a special meaning, namely 'social behavior', 'the way she behaved in the society of others besides Marcher'. Here again, something seems missing. When one 'gives an account of oneself' one explains one's behaviour; but which behaviour, the apparent or the real? Here what seems meant is that May's social behaviour gave a false account of her real behaviour, that is, her dealings with Marcher, so there is at least ellipsis of the idea of 'real' at the end of the sentence. As for 'behaviour', it is not so much that there is ellipsis of an explanatory phrase, but rather that the one offered, 'in the social sense', is displaced; one might argue additionally, however, that since it is the *term* 'behaviour' that is under discussion, there is some ellipsis of quotation marks. Certainly, 'and "behaviour", in the social sense (of the word), had become for her . . .' would have been much clearer.

But then how to explain the shift from 'account of herself' to 'account of her' in the next sentence. The grammar argues an account given by someone *other* than May herself, an account in the abstract, indeed, *the* true account, which May herself is not in a position to give. The reason for her incapacity again, is elided, and must be surmised; she didn't really know why she was so absorbed in his fate and we guess that it is love; she could hardly admit that to herself, let alone to Marcher. 'Directly' sets up its own little eddy: she couldn't have given the account of her feelings directly, but the inference is strong that she could and even did do so indirectly, and that it was precisely Marcher's moral obtuseness and self-absorption that kept him from recognition.

This is verified in the next sentence, a welcome bit of redundance: 'Her whole attitude (toward him, toward the relation) was a virtual statement (of her feelings, of her love) . . .' The rest of this sentence strikes one as a terribly elaborate equivalent of 'but he didn't perceive it', where 'it' like 'that' refers, probably, to the elided object of 'statement' than to the whole clause; however, since the one really includes the other, there's no reason to argue for fine distinctions. (That is, if Marcher had been conscious of her love, he would also have been aware that her attitude was evidence of that love, and, conversely, if he had known that her attitude was evidence of her love, he would also have known that she was in love.)

The following sentence is made difficult by 'their real truth'. 'Their' can be taken as either (or both) objective and subjective genitive: 'the real truth about them' or the like, and also 'the real truth which they possessed'. At the same time, 'real truth' is not as portentous as it seems. It can only be another reference to what they actually talk about in contrast to what society thinks they talk about; since Marcher is 'making sacrifices to it', he must know what it is, and if he knows what is, it is hardly the 'real truth' in any profound sense, say, the 'real truth' about her feelings for him, or the 'real truth' about the beast in his jungle. Then there is an ellipsis after 'compensation'. What compensation did she have? Presumably the opportunity of being with him. But how about the ellipsis of the comparative which follows? Is it 'than his compensation?' (in which case 'if' means 'through')? Or is the emphasis thrown on 'might': '. . . her compensation might have affected her as more prompt and more natural (than it actually did)'? The phrase 'like himself' seems to argue the first, but one's confidence in that interpretation is not very great. Why shouldn't Marcher's 'compensation'—the pleasure of being with an understanding person who knows about his problem—be just as prompt and as natural as May's? Is it that she is infinitely more spontaneous ('prompt') and 'natural' (normal in her capacity for affection)? Once again, with the best will in the world and after more than a little effort, the reader finds himself a bit lost in the portent of it all. But isn't that the point? Isn't it precisely the subtle, uncertain, heavy relationship between these two characters, shy and deferential and highly bred as they are, that James is depicting? Didn't the ends finally justify the means?

That this elliptical effect was positively intended and not simply allowed to slip into the later style is demonstrated by the fact that many of the changes in *Roderick Hudson* introduced ellipsis of one kind or another. For example, in Chapter Nine, after the statement that not only Christina Light but *any* girl 'would have answered Roderick's sentimental needs', the original has 'His extraordinary success in modelling the bust of the beautiful Miss Light was pertinent evidence of this amiable quality' (presumably of being easily susceptible to the charms of women); the revision is even more elliptical: 'His success ... was pertinent evidence of the quantity of consciousness of the great feminine fact always at his service for application and discrimination.' Who is applying what to what, or discriminating what from what? Many other examples can be cited, for example, in the original, 'Christina and Roderick exchanged a single glance—a glance brilliant on each arm'; in the revision, it is 'a glance caught by Rowland and which attested on the part of each to something of a new consciousness'. Consciousness of what? Of Roderick's bust, the original says 'it was a representation of ideal beauty'; the revision complicates the picture with transitive verbs whose objects are deleted: the bust 'succeeded by an exquisite art in representing without extravagance something that transcended and exceeded'. When Christina tells Rowland that she would give anything for a friend, the original wonders 'Was this touching sincerity or unfathomable coquetry?' but the revision asks 'Was this a sincere yearning or only an equivocal purpose?'

Many of the quotation marks that James strews about so freely
involve a kind of ellipsis, in particular, those which are added to
make otherwise simple words 'pregnant'. For example, '. . . there
was in all dissipation . . . a vulgarity which would disqualify it for
Roderick's favor' becomes in the later version '. . . in almost any
crudity of "pleasure" . . .' The implication of the quotation marks is
that it is a 'so-called' pleasure—fashionable, acceptable, perhaps,
but still slightly off-colour. It is the word that devotees would use.
Compare the 'pregnant' quotation marks on 'fate' in 'You're
not our young lady's "fate" ' (for the earlier 'Christina is not for
you') or 'She was not, as Rowland conceived her, the "type"
that . . . would have most touched him' (for the earlier 'She was
not . . . the sort of girl he would have been likely to fancy').

16. HYPERBOLE

I have already mentioned the relation of intangible language to
hyperbole in James. Abstract words tend to overdramatize and
inflate perfectly ordinary actions to which they are applied, hence
they carry strong hyperbolic overtones. One result of the abstract
language is a kind of portentousness, which, as Mr. Watt has
pointed out, has its ironic side. Since the intangible words lose
much of their ordinary intellectual substance, James constantly
risks the accusation that he is merely dressing up the trivialities
of high society in fancy terminology. Strether's reluctance to
meet Waymarsh is inflated into a 'principle' and a 'happy device'.
He doesn't simply intend to preserve his early European memories—he has a 'theory' about preserving them. It isn't merely that
Maggie feels that she is successful in 'abandoning' Amerigo and
Charlotte: she 'holds fast . . . the theory of her success'. Her
acceptance of the 'manner in which she, Charlotte, the Prince and
father lived' becomes a 'process': 'There would be a process of
her own by which she might do differently in respect to Amerigo

and Charlotte—a process quite independent of any process of theirs . . .' (it's no easy thing to figure out what *their* process is). It is not simply that Milly finds Lord Mark frivolous; 'ideas', 'designations', 'connexions', 'classes', 'affinities', and 'elements' have to be introduced:

The idea of his frivolity had, no doubt, to do with his personal desig-nation, which represented—as yet, for our young woman, a little confusedly—a connexion with an historic patriciate, a class that in turn, also confusedly, represented an infinity with a social element she had never heard otherwise described than as 'fashion'.

Mr. Watt has shown the ironic consequences of adding negatives and qualifications to hyperbolical words in a kind of characteristic mock-scrupulousness: 'On [Strether's] learning that Waymarsh was not to arrive till evening, he was not wholly disconcerted', illustrates that 'There are limits to Lambert Strether's consterna-tion'.[1]

But these portentous words are often as much a source of vigour as are James' metaphors. The whole scale of mental action is moved to a higher pitch. For example, in *The Tragic Muse*, 'Lady Agnes substituted a general vague assent to all further particular ones and, with her daughters, withdraw from Mrs. Booth and from the rest of the company'. Though Lady Agnes' assent is 'vague' and 'general', though the action is itself quite unspecified, it is handled, through the verb 'substitute', with something of that lady's characteristic vigour, decision, and command. James' forte was to make the vagaries of society an engaging and even exciting affair, and hyperbole is one of his chief means for doing so.

17. COLLOQUIAL ELEMENTS

Several critics have noted the curious mixture of colloquial and formal diction in James; D. W. Jefferson, for example, writes that

[1] Watt, p. 478.

'The combination of the rhetorical with the colloquial and personal give extraordinary potency and appeal to many passages in James' late work',[1] and R. W. Short compares the 'dense, prefigured, nubilous' aspects of the style with the 'informal and whimsical'. Not only dialogue but also narration, description, and the representation of consciousness may be phrased colloquially. For example, in his revisions James converted every verb negation with 'not' into a contraction with *n't*, and he regularly deleted *that* from sentences like 'I saw that you were there.'

Perhaps most characteristic of James' colloquialisms are the racy two-word verbs, often used metaphorically: 'have (things) out with (somebody)', 'take (somebody or something) in', 'pull (somebody) up', 'have (somebody) in', 'run (something) down', 'cast about (for something)', 'turn (something) in', 'knock about', 'take (something) up', 'put (something) off', and so on and on through literally hundreds of forms. Their occurrences in straight narrative (not dialogue) are frequent. For example, in describing the effects of remarks on characters: 'He couldn't piece it together'; 'It pulled him up a little'; 'She took him up . . . on a minor question', and so on. It is particularly interesting to see them combined with intangibles: '[Strether] had fallen back on the thought that . . .'; 'it enabled his eyes to make out as much of a case for her . . . as her own made out for himself'; 'when [Strether had looked at his watch] for the fifth time, she took him up' [note, too, the breezy ellipsis]. Milly observes wryly to herself 'that there might be a good deal they [she and Lord Mark] would get round to'; 'Milly made out these things—with a shade of exhilaration at the way she already fell in . . .'; 'She asked herself if her right hand neighbour would understand what she meant by such a description of them, should she throw it off . . .'; Lord Mark tells her 'how little he could clear up her situation'; 'she was more and more sharply conscious of having . . . been popped into the compartment in which she was to travel for him' (note how the metaphor is invigorated by the two-word form). From *The*

[1] D. W. Jefferson, *Henry James and the Modern Reader* (Edinburgh, 1964), p. 145.

H

Golden Bowl: 'the truth of it shone out to her like the beauty of a
family picture'; 'it was enough of a recognition for her that,
whatever the thing he might desire, he would always absolutely
bring it off'; 'it had been, for all the world, as if Charlotte had been
"had in", as the servants always said of extra help . . .'; and so on.
Some of these forms are *so* racy, so much a part of ephemeral
upper-class slang, that it is difficult at a distance of sixty years to
be positive about their meaning: 'Lord Mark had been brought
to her before dinner—not by Mrs. Lowder, but by the handsome
girl, that lady's niece, who was now at the other end and on the
same side as Susie; he had taken her in. . .'. 'Take in' in this case
doesn't seem to mean 'fool', nor 'provide a home for her', nor
'introduce her into a place'; perhaps it is 'greet her, accept her,
welcome her to his society, make contact with her', but it also
might mean 'look her over, examine her carefully'.

The two-word verb is made up of simpler, semantically cruder
elements than what it represents as a whole. The elements are
usually simple physical actions—'give, bring, put, take'—to which
are added certain particles. Thus, the separate parts of 'put upon'
or 'bring up' are more primitive than the resultant phrases, but
some of the plain vigour of their separate meanings is preserved.
The use of such combinations in preference to more sophisticated
synonyms—like 'befool' or 'victimize'—does give the style a
racier, more colloquial flavour without a sacrifice in meaning;
and what is characteristically Jamesian is combining them with
high-flown intangible nouns. The result is another kind of
esthetic foregrounding.

There are other colloquial elements as well. We are told that
there is the danger that Strether's 'business' will be 'bungled';
that he doesn't know Maria's friends, the Munsters, well enough
'to give the case much of a lift'; that his glasses are 'eternal
nippers'. Merton finds Susan Stringham 'excited, as in the native
phrase, keyed-up, to a perception of more elements in the occasion
than he was himself able to count'; Lord Mark's 'easy, and after
all, friendly jibe at her race was really for her, on her new friend's
part, the note of personal recognition so far as she required it';

'since Amerigo is amused by English slang expressions like "the straight tip" '. Colloquial elements are very widespread in James, and represent his closest ties with the actual sounds made by the society he so studiously observed.

18. METAPHOR

Finally, and perhaps most importantly, there is the relation between intangibility and metaphor. There has been much discussion of James' metaphors. A recent assessment is that of D. W. Jefferson: 'Some of James' imagery, examined by quasi-metaphysical standards, would emerge with high credit: but in general the approach is mistaken, and many of his finest flourishes would fare no better at the hands of certain critics than the great similes of *Paradise Lost*.'[1] But, of course, that's not the point; James' metaphors, like much in his writing, are not there for a poetic purpose, but for illustration, exemplification, explanation, elaboration, and so on. Jefferson is more germane when he speaks of '. . . James' gift of bringing together the contrasting values of imagery and abstract formulation, so that situations intellectually stated glow or reverberate, or find expression in portentous gesture . . .' The theory is apparently that metaphors can make abstractions so lively that the reader will enjoy them. Maggie 'in the garden of thought' is found 'plucking her plan out of the heart of her earnestness'; her plan is the 'flower of participation' (i.e., greater participation in the social life of her family). 'Participation' is a big abstracted lump of activity—acting as hostess at teas, going to the opera, engaging 'bores' in conversation, and so on; the lump would, presumably, be less digestible without the seasoning of metaphor.

Not the least important fact to be noted about James' metaphors is their great number, a fact which might be obscured by

[1] Jefferson, p. 143.

a preoccupation with unusual or particularly fresh metaphors. Many of James' metaphors are 'low-grade', dé jà vues, familiar to the point of triteness. Again his introduction of them into the revised novels shows that his practice was deliberate. For example, the commonplaces 'flesh and the devil' and 'temple of faith' are substituted for non-metaphorical expressions in the revision of *Roderick Hudson*: the earlier 'He implied in every phrase that he had done with licentious experiments and that he was counting the hours till he should get back to work' becomes 'He conveyed in every phrase that he had done with the flesh and the devil and was counting the hours till he should re-enter the true temple of his faith.' Why should a great writer like James indulge in commonplace or even trite metaphors? I think because his purpose is precisely not poetic; he is concerned with the tissue of society and the psychology of those who live in it. An inescapable part of society is speech, *current* speech, and of course it is the dead and dying metaphors that are on everybody's lips, not fresh, unusual, literary ones.

It is worth James' while to dally with clichés since they are instances of the real contemporary voice, the narrator's as well as the characters'.[1] But it is also characteristic that he should reanimate these by extension and elaboration. This art can be seen clearly, again, in the revisions. In the original *Roderick Hudson*, for example, Mary is simply 'applying herself to a piece of needlework with conscious intentness'; in the revision the trite expression 'sunk up to the chin' is renovated: 'Mary was sunk, up to her firm chin, in one of her eternal pretexts for the fine needle and the occupied attention.' (Note that 'pretexts' is abstract—it doesn't mean 'remarks made by Mary by way of pretext'—and that the nominal phrase 'the occupied attention' is one of those radical Jamesian reductions of a whole clause—'her "pretext" was that embroidery occupied her whole attention', or the like.)

The increase in low-level metaphor in the revisions of the early novels is enormous: within two pages of *The American*, I find

[1] See also the discussion of metaphors in L. Richardson, *Henry James Representative Selections* (New York, 1941), p. ix.

nine metaphors introduced. For example, in the original, Newman's memory of Mr. Babcock's birthplace simply 'assumed in
his mind a jocular cast'; in the revision it 'pressed the spring of
mirth'. Instead of saying 'fellow travelers very soon grow intimate', the revision makes them 'cling together'. Instead of asking
himself whether he should 'associate with our hero', Mr. Babcock
asks whether he should 'give himself up to him'. Rather than
merely 'liking' Newman, he feels himself 'drawn to him'. He
doesn't merely 'form a partnership', he 'falls into' one, and instead of 'taking his leave', he finally 'breaks away'. What characterizes all these metaphors is their reference to simple physical
action as the vehicle. It is as if the loss of contact with the physical
world that James' preoccupation with abstractions and the inner
life entailed was to be recaptured in metaphor.

But my basic concern is the relation between metaphor and
intangibility. Earlier I hazarded the opinion that metaphors were
often introduced by James to enliven what would otherwise be
dry-as-dust exposition, a set of existential statements with abstractions tied together by the copula. There are two principal
ways in which his abstractions are metaphorized. One is simple
noun for noun replacement, for example, memories become
seeds: 'Buried for long years in dark corners, at any rate, these
few germs had sprouted again under forty-eight hours of Paris.'
Old experiments become ghosts: 'Old ghosts of experiments
came back to him, old drudgeries and delusions and disgusts
. . .' Or a recognition becomes a spring: 'The special spring
that had constantly played for him the day before was the recognition . . . of promises to himself that . . . he had never kept.'

But even more interesting is metaphor of the verb, the more
direct way of attacking the problem of excessive use of the copula.
The metaphoric verbs animate and sometimes even personify
abstract nouns which are their subjects. Strether's 'drift was to the
other side and it floated him unspent up the Rue de Seine . . .';
'the cup of his impressions overflowed'; 'It filled for him, this
tone of hers, all the air, yet it struck him at the same time as the
hum of vain things'. Coming to a conclusion is wonderfully

described in terms of butterfly or bee: 'He at last lighted on a form that was happy.' The 'low-grade' physical metaphors are very often used for cognition. Thinking becomes visceral: '. . . could he only maintain with sufficient firmness his grasp of this truth, it might become in a manner his compass and his helm'; 'The long ache might at last drop to rest'; 'The fact that he had failed . . . stood solidly for a crowded past'. Susan Stingham senses a loss of literary inspiration: 'The sustaining sense of it all . . . quite dropped from her'; '. . . explanations would have taken [Milly] much too far'; 'her attention attached itself more and more to the handsome girl'; 'Lord Mark took her for granted . . . and it wouldn't in the least help that she herself knew him, as quickly, for having been in her country and threshed it out.' *The Golden Bowl* is filled with examples: '. . . only that quantity itself escaped . . . familiar naming and discussing'; 'The conditions facing her had yielded . . . to the golden mist'; 'Preparation and practice had come but a short way; her part opened out . . .'; 'The earlier elements flushed into life again'; 'Charlotte's attitude had, in short, its moment of flowering into pretty excesses of civility . . .'; 'his instinct for relations . . . prompted him immediately to meet and match the difference'; 'This new perception bristled for her . . . with odd intimations'; 'Then it was that the dismissed vision of Amerigo . . . this immense little memory gave out its full power'; 'Her thought . . . arrived at a great intensity'. Many of the metaphors introduced into the revised version of *Roderick Hudson* are of the verb: for example, James changed 'At this point of his friend's narrative . . .' to read 'As his friend's narrative sailed closer'. The remark applied to the painter Sam Singleton—that he was 'rioting on chiaroscura'—was intensified to 'making violent love to opportunity'. And 'There was something uncommonly hard to explain in the fact of [Roderick's] falling in love with his cousin' was changed to read 'There was something that mocked any sense of due sequences in the fact of his falling in love with his cousin'.

19. PARODIES OF JAMES' STYLE: AN EVALUATION

One of the best, and certainly one of the more amusing ways of studying a style is through parodies. Whether as successes or failures, they cannot but be instructive. The method is clear: if a feature—say the intangible noun or nominalization as sentence-topic—occurs frequently in the original we expect to find many examples in a successful parody, too. An unsuccessful parody will fail, in part, by not recognizing such a feature; the parodist will be guilty of the error of omission. But he may also be guilty of the opposite fault, the error of commission. Of course, in a substantial corpus, practically any feature is bound to occur at least once; but dwelling upon something which is not typical or characteristic, which does not make us think of the original, as opposed to some other style, is clearly a fault.

What is true of the parody is equally true of its stylistic analysis; if the analysis is good, it should be able to account for successes and failures in the parody as well as the character of the original, not vaguely but exactly, in terms of specific features.

There have been several parodies of James' style, but I shall consider only two, a good one, by Max Beerbohm, and a fairly bad one, by W. H. D. Rouse.[1] The first has as its subject the awarding of the Order of Merit to James. It depicts in a delightful way the vague confusions of the King and his Lord Chamberlain, Stamfordham, about James' identity.

[1] Max Beerbohm, 'The Guerdon', in *Parodies: An Anthology*, 147-9, and W. H. D. Rouse, 'The Enchanted Copse', in 'Style', *Essays and Studies*, XXVII (1941), 52-65.

THE GUERDON

That it hardly was, that it all bleakly and unbeguilingly *wasn't* for 'the likes' of *him*—poor decent Stamfordham—to rap out queries about the owner of the to him unknown and unsuggestive name that had, in these days, been thrust on him with such a wealth of commendatory gesture, was precisely what now, as he took, with his prepared list of New Year *colifichets* and whatever, his way to the great gaudy palace, fairly flicked his cheek with the sense of his having never before so let himself in, as he ruefully phrased it, without letting anything, by the same token, out.

'Anything' was, after all, only another name for *the* thing. But he was to ask himself what earthly good it was, anyhow, to have kept in its confinement the furred and clawed, the bristling and now all but audibly scratching domestic pet, if he himself, defenseless Lord Chamberlain that he was, had to be figured as bearing it company inside the bag. There wasn't, he felt himself blindly protesting, room in there for the two of them; and the imminent addition of a Personage fairly caused our friend to bristle in the manner of the imagined captive that had till now symbolised well enough for him his whole dim bland ignorance of the matter in hand. Hadn't he all the time been reckoning precisely *without* that Personage—*without* the greater dimness that was to be expected of *him*—without, above all, that dreadful lesser blandness in virtue of which such personages tend to come down on you, as it were, straight, with demands for side-lights? There wasn't a 'bally' glimmer of a side-light, heaven help him, that he could throw. He hadn't the beginning of a notion—since it had been a point of pride with him, as well as of urbanity, not to ask—who the fellow, the so presumably illustrious and deserving chap in question *was*. This omission so loomed for him that he was to be conscious, as he came to the end of the great moist avenue, of a felt doubt as to whether he could, in his bemusement, now 'place' anybody at all; to which condition of his may have been due the impulse that, at the reached gates of the palace, caused him to pause and all vaguely, all peeringly inquire of one of the sentries: 'To whom do you beautifully belong?'

The question, however, was to answer itself, then and there, to the effect that this functionary belonged to whom *he* belonged to; and the converse of this reminder, presenting itself simultaneously to his consciousness, was to make him feel, when he was a few minutes later ushered into the Presence, that he had never so intensely, for general abjectness and sheer situational funk, belonged as now. He caught himself wondering whether, on this basis, he were even animate, so strong was his sense of being a 'bit' of the furniture of the great glossy 'study'—of being some oiled and ever so handy object moving smoothly on castors, or revolving, at the touch of a small red royal finger, on a pivot. It would be placed questioningly, that finger—and his pre-vision held him as with the long-drawn pang of nightmare—on the cryptic name. That it occurred, this name, almost at the very end of the interminable list, figured to him not as a respite but as a prolongment of the perspirational agony. So that when, at long last, that finger *was* placed, with a roll towards him of the blue, the prominent family eye of the seated reader, it was with a groan of something like relief that he faintly uttered an 'Oh well, Sir, he *is*, you know—and with all submission, hang it, just *isn't* he though?—of an eminence!'

It was in the silence following this fling that there budded for him the wild, the all but unlooked-for-hope that 'What *sort*, my dear man, of eminence?' was a question not, possibly, going to be asked at all. It fairly burst for him and blossomed, this bud, as the royal eye rolled away from his into space. It never, till beautifully now, had struck our poor harrassed friend that his master might, in some sort, be prey to those very, those inhibitive delicacies that had played, from first to last, so eminently the deuce with *him*. He was to see, a moment later, that the royal eye had poised—had, from its slow flight around the mouldings of the florid Hanoverian ceiling, positively swooped— on the fat scarlet book of reference which, fraught with a title that was a very beam of the catchy and the chatty, lay beside the blotting-pad. The royal eye rested, the royal eye even dilated, to such an extent that Stamfordham had anticipatively the sense of being commanded to turn for a few minutes his back, and of overhearing in that interval the rustle of the turned leaves.

That no such command came, that there *was* no recourse to the dreadful volume, somewhat confirmed for him his made guess that on the great grey beach of the hesitational and renunciational he was not—or wasn't all deniably not—the only pebble. For an instant, nevertheless, during which the prominent blue eye rested on a prominent blue pencil, it seemed that this guess might be, by an immense *coup de roi*, terrifically shattered. Our friend held, as for an eternity, his breath. He was to form, in later years, a theory that the name really *had* stood in peril of deletion, and that what saved it was that the good little man, as doing, under the glare shed by his predecessors, the great dynastic 'job' in a land that had been under two Jameses and no less than eight Henrys, had all humbly and meltingly resolved to 'let it go at that'.

Rouse's parody is one of several he composed to illustrate well-known English prose styles (Gibbon, Carlyle, and Macaulay, as well as James), using as common content Mr. Jingle's story of his sagacious dog.[1]

THE ENCHANTED COPSE

It might almost perhaps have been one of those strangely if artistically and impressively carved figures of stone, basalt one would say or granite, for the colour varied from gray-brown to a reddish as of gingerbread, which one may come upon in the forests of Mexico, where the Aztecs used to, so at least I gather from history, congregate about their rock-hewn altars to propitiate some polysyllabic deity; for he stood as if petrified by some superhuman power, immovable as the Matterhorn, like a person without an alternative, immersed in immobility up to the chin. The bristling hard hairs that stood up on his narrow forehead pointed as it were upwards as postulating one might conceive a sort of power from above which had caused this sudden denial of all previous reciprocities and obediences, when he would come at a call unregarding any extraneous temptations or constraints; and yet his eyes, or rather his eye, the companion orb having been put out by a chance shot from a friend's gun, who I need hardly say was never again solicited to join our peregrinations, was fixed in a stony stare on some object not visible to me, situated no

---

[1] From *The Pickwick Papers*:

Ah—you should keep dogs—fine animals—sagacious creatures—dog of my own once—pointer—surprising instinct—out shooting one day—entering enclosure—whistled—dog stopt—whistled again—Ponto—no go—stock still—called him—Ponto, Ponto—wouldn't move—dog transfixed—staring at a board—looked up—saw an inscription—Gamekeeper has orders to shoot all dogs found in the enclosure—wouldn't pass it—wonderful dog—valuable dog that—very.

doubt on one of the contradictious architectural overarchings of the boughs. And to further confuse the ratiocinating movements of Supposition, his tail stuck out in a straight line with his body but in a direction diametrically opposed to his gaze, the member which gave a name to his useful and intelligent breed, as pointing stiff at something, it may be his master, while his thoughts, for they are thoughtful beyond the lot of fourfooted creatures, pointed ahead to the game which his master sought.

I had called him by name, and whistled more than once, thrice in fact if it is important to indicate all the minutiae, so that no reader may ever for one moment hesitate as to what psychological process was taking, one may say, place in the, shall we call them minds, of the various characters and personalities whose actions and reactions compose the subject-, as one might call it, matter of what may not improperly be described as the novelist's immortal work. Yet to this threefold invitation there was no response; and I, who had set forth with Ponto to discover, if discovery were possible, something to, if the means were well adjusted to the end, shoot, had entered the wood, and imagining the possible or even probable presence of something fit for that purpose, had called him to share in my search and provided it were not a fox in my triumph and the preparation for the anticipated dinner. Such a contradiction of all habits and predilections as that this so sagacious, if I may say so, creature should so far from coming not come, but stand petrified gazing at something hidden from me and undisclosed, was too much for my hitherto fixed resolution to shoot something, and I myself retraced my steps and came out of the shadow of the trees, then at the word 'one', turned about face and raised my eyes to the region, where from a calculation of the angle of the sagacious creature's gaze I inferred that as likely to be situated, which had so remarkably and inexplicably attracted his attention. What this was I didn't know, but it was literally as if the reckoning sat there between us, and all the terms we had ever made with felt differences, intensities of separation and opposition, had now been superseded by the need for fresh ones in forms of contact and exchange, forms of pretended intercourse, to be improvised in the presence of new truths. With an effort I was able to gradually and carefully although undissuadably and progressively bring my adequately focussed if I may say so eyes to bear upon the point, and this proved to be no other than one of those publications or indications by which the owners of property discourage those whose natural and inborn tendencies lead them to confuse as conterminate the wholly disterminate considerations which our Roman not exactly forefathers but morally something of the sort distinguished by the surely too brief and inadequately refined disyllables meum and tuum. 'GAMEKEEPER'—thus it began, omitting no doubt for purposes of economy and not to calculatedly and intentionally affront the definite article, or it may be the indefinite, who can tell where all is uncertain,—'HAS ORDERS'—yet from whom was not said, the composer perhaps concealing by this parsimony of information an inferior or non-existent right to give any orders whatsoever—'TO SHOOT'— not as one might expect game of any kind, not even foxes, as perhaps might be looked for from a conscientious objector to hunting, for shooting need not imply hunting, not those who love war as a pacifist might have done, but—'ALL DOGS'—surely a superfluity of supererogance, but stay, there is a qualification which if rightly understood and placed in the balance may or indeed should or must relieve somewhat our too-early aroused apprehensions, 'FOUND IN THE ENCLOSURE', so that as it would manifestly appear it is no crime to *be* in the enclosure or even to *hunt* there, but the crime as so often in human life is to be found out. Now Ponto was 'out', but not yet 'found', and indeed here the crime is to be 'found in', a notable variation on the ordinary course of things. Be that as it may, and it would not 'do' to summarily and without further deliberation finally conclude that all these thoughts has passed through the mind of Ponto, yet one thing is abundantly clear, Ponto could read: an act not usually within the canine accomplishment, which leads me to the reason why I have written all this, namely to say you should keep dogs, they are fine creatures of surprising instinct, and I once had one myself.

Why does Beerbohm's parody seem so much more accurate than Rouse's? My answer shall follow the terms and the order of the discussion above.

Of the twenty-six grammatical subjects of main clauses in 'The Guerdon,' seventeen, or 65 per cent, are abstractions; only seven (27 per cent) refer to humans and only two (8 per cent) refer to things, and even these are more figurative rather than real: the 'bud' in sentence fifteen and the 'royal eye' in eighteen. This is an accurate, even exaggerated (caricatured) display of James' penchant for intangible subjects (see sections 5, 7, 8). Rouse, on the other hand, introduces only seven intangible subjects, out of a possible twenty-four (29 per cent), while human subjects (including the anthropomorphized dog) amount to twelve (50 per cent), and physical objects (mostly body parts) to five (21 per cent): clearly not a Jamesian distribution.

Even more significant than the number are the kinds of abstractions that are included, and what is done (or not done) with them. Most of Beerbohm's sentences contain the classical Jamesian elements: the abstract nominalized subject commanding, often through a dramatic, quasi-metaphorical verb, the mind of the poor human object (compare pp. 111 ff. above)—'his pre-vision held him as with the long-drawn pang of nightmare', 'the converse of this reminder, presenting itself simultaneously to his consciousness, was to make him feel . . .' (note the characteristic reflexive pronoun animating the neuter nouns, see p. 61 above). Sometimes the verb is dressed up in a metaphor: 'This omission so loomed for him that . . .' (compare pp. 111ff. above; 'loom', of course, is one of James' great words—it contains just the right mixture of vagueness and portent, and, at the same time, does no more than announce the presence of something on the scene). Another is '. . . the imminent addition of a Personage fairly caused our friend to bristle . . .' There are many other instances in which the human being is a more or less passive recipient of thoughts and impressions, rather than their active subject: it isn't that Stamfordham merely 'thinks' that it was not for the likes of him to rap out queries and so on, rather the idea fairly 'flicks his cheek' (combining metaphor and synecdoche); it isn't that he 'joins' the cat in the bag, rather he has to be figured as 'doing so' (agent deleted); it isn't that he 'protests', rather he 'feels himself protesting'; nor does he 'refuse' to ask who the fellow is, rather it 'is a point of pride with him . . .' not to do so; it is not simply that he asks the sentry that other wonderful question, there exists, rather, a 'condition of his' to which 'may have been due the impulse' that 'causes him' to ask it; it isn't that he 'discovers' the answer to the question, rather the question 'answers itself' (with deletion of personal reference altogether); he doesn't merely 'wonder', he 'catches himself wondering'; he does not 'hope' that the question would not be asked, but rather there 'buds' for him such a hope. Note in many of these the authentically Jamesian profusion of prepositions to show the oblique personal stance to these abstractions: *for, with, to,* and *in.* Beerbohm clearly understands what has been described by Shriber and elaborated above, namely that James' later fiction characterizes the mental process more frequently as the reception of impressions than as an active performance. It is this that helps to make poor Stamfordham a genuinely Jamesian hero, a pleasantly agonized, passive observer at arm's length of his own thoughts and feelings.

There is little mental action of any kind in Rouse's parody, and what there is tends to be performative rather than recipient: the narrator 'gathers' something from history; he 'imagines' the possibility of something to shoot; he 'infers' the presence of the sign from the angle of the dog's stare; he doesn't 'know' and the dog 'knows that he doesn't know' what it is looking at; and so on. There are only one or two recipient forms, for example, in sentence seven—which for that and other reasons, as we shall see, is the best of Rouse's efforts.

Beerbohm is also successful with deictic and expletive constructions. He not only introduces James' deictic nouns *something-anything* (see p. 54 above), but seasons them with the familiar portentous quotation marks and italicization: ' "Anything" was, after all, only another name for *the* thing.' Further, there are no less than four instances of *that*-clauses as subjects (in the first, twelfth, seventeenth, and eighteenth sentences). That is even a bit many, but then we must allow the parodist's right to caricature. Sentence twelve is particularly interesting, since it contains a superadded anticipatory deixis: 'That it occurred, this name, almost at the very end of the interminable list, figured to him not as a respite but as a prolongment of the perspirational agony.' Like its original, too, the style of Beerbohm's parody is laden with sentences beginning with expletive or 'cleft' *it* (see above pp. 72 ff.). Beerbohm's ear is particularly delicate in catching the construction with preposition: '. . . it was with a groan of something like relief that he faintly uttered . . .' and 'It was in the silence following this fling that . . .' There are no instances of the *what*-cleft in the subject, but there is one in complement function: 'That it hardly was . . . for "the likes" of *him* . . . was precisely what now . . . fairly flicked his cheek . . .' Similarly, Beerbohm recognizes the widespread use of the *there* expletive: 'There wasn't . . . room . . .', 'There wasn't a . . . glimmer'; and even more characteristic, with a non-copulative verb: 'There budded for him the . . . hope that . . .' There is also the Jamesian pure adjective as nominal (see p. 49): the scarlet book of reference has a title that is 'the very beam of the catchy and the chatty'; similarly, Stamfordham finds that the King is another pebble on 'the great grey beach of the hesitational and renunciational'. Beerbohm has also mastered the Jamesian gerundive construction (see p. 26 above): 'he had to be figured as bearing it company . . .', 'the sense of his having never before so let himself in . . . without letting anything . . . out', 'so strong was his sense of being a "bit" of the furniture . . .', 'the sense of being commanded to turn . . . his back' (note the frequency of 'sense').

There are little of these riches in Rouse's parody. He introduces only two abstract nouns as subjects, 'contradiction' and 'crime', and only the first is a nominalization (on the strength of that word alone the sixth sentence, along with the seventh, is more validly Jamesian than the others). Rouse does use *it* and *there* constructions frequently, however; he even recognizes the Jamesian penchant for 'It was as if . . .' (not included by Beerbohm), introducing the best of his efforts:

. . . it was literally as if the reckoning sat there between us, and all the terms we had ever made with felt differences, intensities of separation and opposition, had now been superseded by the need for fresh ones in forms of contact and exchange, forms of pretended intercourse, to be improvised in the presence of new truths.

Here are enough abstractions to satisfy the Jamesian taste— many of them nominalizations, and some even in plural or 'mass' forms without definite articles (see pp. 81 ff.); there is the homely compensatory metaphor of the verb 'sat'; there are Jamesisms like 'forms', 'intensities', and so on; there is widespread ellipsis ('contact' and 'exchange' of what? 'truths' about what?); there are even agentless past-participial modifiers ('felt differences', 'pretended intercourse', see p. 38). Unfortunately, Rouse's other sentences, despite occasional touches, are much inferior to this one. Often what starts out convincingly enough with a nominalization of the real verb and obliquing or omission of subjects and objects—for example: '. . . which had caused this sudden denial of all previous reciprocities and obediences', a Jamesian effect if left at that, particularly the naked plural abstractions—gets spoiled by unnecessary overexplicitness—'. . . when he would come at a call unregarding any extraneous temptations or constraints . . .' James would have left to the reader the task of spelling out the 'reciprocities' and 'obediences'; an explanatory clause is precisely what he would not have included.

Beerbohm shows his mastery of Jamesian ellipsis in several sentences. In the first sentence, for example, is it that he is 'letting himself in *for* something' (though that wouldn't explain 'letting anything . . . out'); or that it is the 'bag' he has let himself into, and 'anything' is the cat? Similarly, about the 'lesser blandness', specifically pointed to with a 'that', no clarification is offered. Like James, Beerbohm frequently introduces ellipses at the very ends of sentences, where it pulls the reader up especially short, for example: '. . . with demands for sidelights'. Or with deletion of the direct object: 'he had never so intensely . . . belonged as now'. Or, with deletion of personal reference, 'a prolongment of the perspirational agony'. He also has caught James' habit of using *as* as a preposition introducing a phrase instead of as a conjunction introducing a clause: 'his pre-vision held him as with the long-drawn pang of nightmare'; 'our friend held, as for an eternity, his breath'; 'the good little man, as doing . . . the great dynastic "job" . . .' Rouse manages this kind of ellipsis only once, in his second sentence, which is otherwise not very good ('. . . pointed as it were upwards as postulating . . . one might conceive . . .' etc.).

Beerbohm is by far the more accurate, too, in his imitation of the pecularities of Jamesian word order. He produces many instances of that interruption and partial repetition that is endemic in the later style. Since I have not mentioned this important feature before, let me offer a random example, from James, a sentence that occurs early in *A Round of Visits* (1910): 'He so felt the blow, indeed so gasped, before what had happened to him, at the ugliness, the bitterness, and, beyond these things, the sinister strangeness, that, the matter of his dismay little by little detaching and projecting itself, settling there face to face with him as something he must now live with always, he might have been in charge of some horrible alien thing, some violent, scared, unhappy Creature . . .' Note the repetition and halt of the constructions with 'so', and of the objects of 'gasped at', of 'detaching', 'projecting', and 'settling', and of 'some . . . thing', and 'some . . . Creature'. Many examples of this sort of thing can be found in Beerbohm's parody. For example: 'That it hardly was, that it all bleakly and unbeguilingly *wasn't* . . .'; 'the furred and clawed, the bristling and now all but audibly scratching domestic pet'; 'to pause and all vaguely, all peeringly inquire of one of the sentries'; 'of being a "bit" of the furniture . . . of being some oiled and ever so handy object'; 'the blue, the prominent family eye'; 'those very, those inhibitive delicacies'; 'the royal eye had poised, had positively swooped'; 'the royal eye rested, the royal eye even dilated'. Rouse not only fails to perceive this feature but introduces an alternative whose top-heaviness James would never have tolerated: 'one of those strangely if artistically and impressively carved figures of stone, basalt one would say or granite' (not 'one of those strangely, one of those artistically . . .' etc.). Beerbohm is also handy with what I have called anticipatory or French deixis (see p. 63 above): 'it would be placed questioningly, that finger', 'it . . . *wasn't* for "the likes" of *him*—poor decent Stamfordham', 'that it occurred, this name', 'it fairly burst for him . . . this bud'. Again, Rouse was apparently quite unaware of this feature.

It is true that Rouse often makes motions in the direction of the

I

Jamesian disruptive interpolation, but his efforts are not very successful. Consider for example, his fourth sentence:

I had called him by name, and whistled more than once, thrice in fact if it is important to indicate all the minutiae, so that no reader may even for one moment hesitate as to what psychological process was taking, one may say, place in the, shall we call them minds, of the various characters and personalities whose actions and reactions compose the subject-, as one might call it, matter of what may not improperly be described as the novelist's immortal work.

This is heavy-handed, even flat-footed, and the errors are as much in the form as in the content. For all its implied bizarreness (for example, the separation of the two parts of the compound 'subject-matter'), it is not really typical of the Jamesian interruption. The main structure ends as early as 'once', and the rest is simply tacked on, as trailing modification. Linguists would call this a heavily right-branching sentence, that is, one in which the modifiers occur *after* the main structure is completed (as opposed to left-branching ones, in which they occur *before*). But, as has been shown recently by Richard Ohmann,[1] James' structures are typically *self-embedded* rather than branching. Ohmann's example is the first sentence of *The Bench of Desolation*: 'She had practically, he believed, conveyed the intimation, the horrid, brutal, vulgar menace, in the course of their last dreadful conversation, when, for whatever was left him of pluck or confidence—confidence in what he would fain have called a little more aggressively the strength of his position—he had judged best not to take it up.' Of this passage Ohmann writes:

. . . notice that most of [the] complexity results from self-embedding. With the embedded elements removed the sentence is still far from simple, but the Jamesian intricacy is gone:

She had practically conveyed the intimation in the course of their last dreadful conversation when he had judged best not to take it up.

[1] In 'Generative Grammars and the Concept of Literary Style', *Word*, XX (1964), pp. 436-7.

The following are the deleted sentences, with their full structure restored:

He believed [it].
[The intimation was a] horrid,
brutal, vulgar menace.
[Something] was left him of pluck or
confidence.
[It was] confidence in the strength
of his position.
He would fain have called [it that],
a little more aggressively.

The embedded elements, in short, significantly outweigh the main sentence itself, and needless to say, the strain on attention and memory required to follow the progress of the main sentence over and around so many obstacles is considerable. The difficulty, as well as the Jamesian flavor, is considerably lessened merely by substituting left- and right-branching constructions for self-embedding, even though all the kernel sentences are retained:

He believed that in the course of their last dreadful conversation she had practically conveyed the intimation, a horrid, brutal, vulgar menace, which he had then judged best not to take up, for whatever was left him of pluck or confidence—confidence in the strength of his position, as he would fain have called it, a little more agressively.

It seems likely that much of James' later style can be laid to this syntactic device—a matter of *positioning* various constructions, rather than of favoring a few particular constructions.

(The sentence from *A Round of Visits*, quoted immediately above, demonstrates the same tendency.)

Yet it is not only embedding but embedding with ellipsis that makes James' style so difficult. In the sentence from *The Bench of Desolation*: who are 'she' and 'he' and 'it'? 'Intimation' and 'menace' of what? 'Position' in reference to what? The ellipsis additionally taxes the reader's ingenuity and memory. The verb phrase 'had conveyed' is first interrupted by two elements, but it is not only that the longish appositional phrase occurs immediately after 'intimation', but that 'intimation' is never completed—we wait helplessly for a clause or phrase to clear things up—'intimation of what' or 'intimation that what'? When no overt completion occurs, we have to allow for one (as we allow for the past participle in a long German sentence) to make some sort of sense of things. We have to hold open a mental slot for that intimation or menace, and we may spend a few moments speculating about what it might be. Thereafter, the *when*-construction, of course, is a straightforward (right-branching) modification of 'conversation', but it too is interrupted internally by the appositional phrase 'confidence . . . position', which in turn is interrupted by another elliptical phrase, 'a little more aggressively' ('more aggressively' than what? or than whom?). Thus, it is not only the interruptions that hamper us but the fact that the interruped element is likely not to be resumed.

Rouse's ideas about the kinds of structures within which James introduces interpolations are not particularly accurate. Though James is capable of splitting close-knit syntactic groups, he does not often do so in the *pre*-nominal space, as Rouse frequently suggests: for example: 'in the, shall we call them minds', 'this so sagacious, if I may say so, creature', 'my adequately focussed if I may say so eyes', and the wretched 'our Roman not exactly forefathers but morally something of the sort'. What is much more typical in James is interpolation between verb and complement. Beerbohm is again more accurate: 'Our friend held, as for an eternity, his breath', 'the sense of being commanded to turn for a few minutes his back', 'He was to form, in later years, a theory', 'There wasn't, he felt himself blindly protesting, room in there for the two of them'; or between adjective and complement: 'he was to be conscious, as he came to the end of the great moist avenue, of a felt doubt'; or between auxiliary and main verb 'whether he could, in his bemusement, now "place" anybody at all'. Further, though James may have several interpolations within a given sentence, they do not occur so regularly spaced as Rouse's parody suggests, for example, in his fourth sentence. Following the tendency to embed, James' interpolations more usually cluster in the centre. A random example from *The Ivory Tower*: 'He was a person without an alternative, and if any had ever been open to him, at an odd hour or two, somewhere in his inner dimness, he had long since closed the gate against it . . .' Or another: 'He had over and above that particular matter of her passing perception, he had, as they all had, goodness knew, and as she herself must have done not least, the air of waiting for something he didn't speak of and in fact couldn't know.'

Nor are the contents, of Rouse's interpolations particularly accurate. For one thing, James would never repeat the same phrase within so short a space, as Rouse repeats 'if I may say so', 'no doubt', and 'surely'. More importantly, the function that Rouse's interpolations play is generally wrong: they tend to be *external* to the narrative, that is, they evoke some direct communication between the narrator and the reader, often in the form of an apology or concession about the accuracy of the information or the narrator's right to present it: 'so at least I gather', 'as it were', 'one would say', 'one may say', 'one might conceive', 'a sort of', 'or rather', 'I need hardly say', 'if I may say so', 'it may be', 'so at least I gather', 'no doubt', 'shall we call them', 'as one might call it', 'what may not improperly be described as', 'not exactly . . . but morally something of the sort', 'who can tell where all is uncertain', and the dismal 'thrice in fact if it is important to indicate all the minutiae, so that no reader may even for one moment hesitate as to what psychological process was taking . . . place' (which substitutes commentary for parody, the baldest kind of telling for showing). Or, even worse, his interpolation is editorial, taking the form of a kind of folk or gnomic utterance which James surely would have detested: 'for they [*dogs*] are thoughtful beyond the lot of fourfooted creatures', 'for shooting need not imply hunting', 'the crime as so often in human life is to be found out'. James' interpolations, on the other hand, are usually dramatic, that is, they tend to occur *within* the context of a character's consciousness as he struggles with his problems. Look again at the sentence from *The Ivory Tower* quoted above:

the interpolations are 'over and above that particular matter of his passing perception', 'as they all had', 'goodness knew', 'as she herself must have done not least', 'in fact'. Each is in or related to the character's depicted consciousness, part of the expression by the character, to himself, of emotions ('goodness knows') or of ratiocination (his separation of this matter from that, his recognition that the 'air of waiting for something' applies to others besides himself). Since Jamesian discourse is regularly an interpretation of a character's consciousness—he is his only audience—his exquisite rectifications too must ordinarily be those made to himself. For example, 'goodness knows' is an internal protest in the throes of self-examination that the 'air of waiting' is indeed not his alone. Rouse's failure to understand this is simply part of his larger failure to select the proper narrative point of view; because he chose the first person, it was easy for the narrator-character to slip into a monologue in which he directly addresses his audience (for example, he uses the imperative 'stay' at one point). But one of the reasons that James avoided first person narrative was to disallow that possibility. Beerbohm's interpolations are much more acceptably Jamesian because they are internal to the depiction of the Lord Chamberlain's consciousness: they represent the hero's (not the *narrator's*) emotions ('heaven help him', 'in his bemusement', 'hang it!') or sense of his situation ('defenseless Lord Chamberlain that he was', 'on this basis', 'with all submission'), or of fixing things in space and time ('then and there', 'for a few minutes', 'as for an eternity', 'in later years'). Beerbohm also uses the interpolation, in the characteristic Jamesian way, to remind the reader that this *is* an 'inner view' ('he felt himself blindly protesting', 'as he ruefully phrased it'), a function which I have called the 'authority tag' (see n. 1, page 41).

Beerbohm is also more adept at Jamesian parallelism and antithesis than Rouse, sensing their frequently asymmetric character, in which the second member is longer than the first: 'That it hardly was, that it all bleakly and unbeguilingly *wasn't* for the "likes" of *him* . . .', 'let himself in . . . without letting anything by the same token out', 'the bristling and now all but audibly scratching pet'. About all that Rouse has to offer is 'that this . . . creature should so far from coming not come', whose abruptness, stemming from overly short elements and from making the first element longer than the second is not convincingly Jamesian.

In comparison and metaphor, too, Rouse has difficulty sustaining the genuinely Jamesian note. He does manage 'like a person without an alternative', 'immersed in immobility up to the chin', and 'the reckoning sat there between us', with their good mixture of abstract and (tritely) concrete; but his other attempts are quite inaccurate. Things are too often compared to other things: the dog is compared to an Aztec stone figure and the boughs to architectural structures. Nothing in the way of Beerbohm's wonderful revitalization of the cat-in-the-bag cliché, the likening of Stamfordham's problem to 'the furred and clawed, the bristling and now all but audibly scratching domestic pet'. The fanciful elaboration of the banal image is, as we have seen, one of James' great arts. Another cliché that Beerbohm resurrects is 'the only pebble on the beach': 'That no such command came . . . somewhat confirmed for him his made guess that on the great grey beach of the hesitational and renunciational he was not— or wasn't all deniably not—the only pebble.' The vehicle of the dead metaphor takes on colour, though it is only grey, and it is yoked to two resounding adjective-abstractions. Another example is the cliché 'budding hope': 'It was in the silence following this fling that there budded for him the wild, the all but unlooked-for hope that "What *sort*, my dear man, of eminence?" was a question not, possibly, going to be asked at all. It fairly burst for him and blossomed, this bud, as the royal eye rolled away from his into space.'

In good Jamesian style, Beerbohm's metaphors combine the intangible with the physical: 'That it . . . wasn't for "the likes" of him to rap out queries . . . was precisely what now . . . fairly flicked his cheek. . .'. In the same sentence the cleft-*that* construction, a reduced (nominalized) form of a whole sentence-length proposition, becomes a gust of wind or a hurled stone by a metaphoric verb 'flicked his cheek' (see pp. 111 ff. above), an image authentically attenuated at the moment that it is offered up by one of James' favourite intensifiers, *fairly*.

James' penchant for the unusual collocation, the mélange of different dictions—colloquial and portentous, racy and abstract— is well captured in Beerbohm's parody. The effect may be marked or not by quotation marks and italics (the inconsistency is Jamesian too): 'it all bleakly and unbeguilingly *wasn't* for "the likes" of him', 'to rap out queries' (notice the racy two-word verb, discussed above on pp. 107 ff.), 'what earthly good it was to have kept in its confinement the . . . domestic pet', 'that dreadful lesser blandness in virtue of which such Personages tend to come down on you, as it were, straight, with demands for side-lights', 'the so presumably illustrious and deserving chap', 'sheer situational funk', 'his sense of being a "bit" of the furniture', 'some oiled and ever so handy object', 'with all submission, hang it', 'those inhibitive delicacies that had played . . . so eminently the deuce with *him*', 'fraught with a title that was a very beam of the catchy and the chatty', 'the great dynastic "job" '. In Rouse there is none of this unpredictable mixture. Given 'carved', his 'strangely' and 'artistically' are not difficult to predict (the way it is impossible to predict, from 'bleakly' and 'unbeguilingly', Beerbohm's 'the "likes" of *him*', or his 'blandness' from 'dreadful'). Rouse does pile up modifiers without commas in the Jamesian manner— 'bristling hard hairs', 'his useful intelligent breed', 'to gradually and carefully although undissuadably and progressively bring my . . . eyes to bear' (though James does not, I think, split infinitives). But they do not have the odd and quirky Jamesian disparity that we find, for example, in this sentence from *Crapy Cornelia*: 'The tones of the frolic infants ceased to be nondescript and harsh—were in fact almost as fresh and decent as the frilled and puckered and ribboned garb of the little girls, which has always a way, in those parts, of so portentously flaunting the daughters of the strange native—that is of the overwhelming alien—populace for him': 'frolic infants', 'puckered garb', 'portentously flaunting', and so on.

Further, Beerbohm shows himself apt at Jamesian elegant variation (section 14). In addition to personal pronouns, he varies reference to the king by calling him 'Personage', 'Presence', 'seated reader', 'Sir', 'his master', 'the good little man', and by various figures, 'the small red royal finger', 'the royal eye', and a 'pebble'; Stamfordham is 'the Lord Chamberlain', 'my dear man', 'our harrassed friend'; while James is 'the owner of the name', 'the fellow', and 'the deserving chap'. Even the cat has several appellations: 'the domestic pet', 'the imagined captive' and 'the thing'. So far is Rouse from observing this trait that he is guilty of ponderously repeating 'sagacious creature', the only variant on 'Ponto' (except for the synecdoches 'eye' and 'tail'), and the only other name given to 'I' is 'his master'.

Beerbohm achieves other small successes of imitation in syntax and vocabulary, which deserve brief mention. He uses the past participial construction in the strained Jamesian way, to replace a relative clause or the like (see pp. 38 ff. above): 'as he took, with his prepared list of New Year *colifichets* and whatever', 'to which condition of his may have been due the impulse that, at the reached gates of the palace, caused him to pause', 'that no such command came . . . somewhat confirmed for him his made guess that . . .', 'he was to be conscious . . . of a felt doubt'. He introduces Jamesian alliterations and other sorts of phonetic repetition: 'bleakly and unbeguilingly', 'unknown and unsuggestive', 'great gaudy palace', 'fairly flicked'. (Rouse does offer 'immersed in immobility', 'stony stare', 'superfluity of supererogance', but other combinations seem quite unmotivated: 'probable presence', 'propitiate some polysyllabic deity'). Beerbohm also catches James' habit of signalling both present and future time by means of the expression *be to*: 'But he was to ask himself what earthly good it was', 'this omission so loomed for him that he was to be conscious . . .', 'the converse of this reminder . . . was to make him feel', 'He was to see, a moment later, that', 'He was to form, in later years, a theory'. A number of other words and expressions popular with James play a prominent role in Beerbohm's parody: the attenuator 'fairly', already mentioned, 'all' (as intensifier of adjectives and adverbs), 'in these days', 'figure', 'the matter in hand', 'dim', 'side-light', 'loomed', ' "place" ', 'to the effect that', 'caught' or 'felt himself' doing something, 'on this basis', 'in some sort', 'have the sense of' something, and so on.

So far I have spoken mostly of Rouse's sins of omission, but no evaluation of parody can neglect a discussion of those of commission, that is, features introduced which clearly do not represent the style parodied. I have noted that Rouse erroneously depicts James as moving in a fog of words. He attributes uncertainty and vagueness not only to his characters but to the author himself. Though James does introduce uncertainties and vagueness, they are clearly motivated, for example, to achieve the effect of plenitude (see above pp. 78 ff.). But Rouse gives the impression that James himself is confused, that he does not quite know what he means, or what the precise word for a thing is: 'Thus it began, omitting no doubt for purposes of economy and to calculatedly and intentionally affront the definite article, or it may be the indefinite, who can tell where all is uncertain . . .', 'our Roman not exactly forefathers but morally something of the sort', and so on. Further, he implies that James is repetitious or redundant. This is particularly inexact; if anything, as we have seen in ample detail, James often risks obscurity by eliminating ordinarily necessary redundancies, the objects of transitive verbs and other vital sentence elements. He would never be guilty of virtual reduplications like 'characters and personalities', 'hidden from me and undisclosed' (whose word order is Miltonic, not Jamesian), 'publications or indications' (both redundant and vague, because of 'or'), 'natural and inborn tendencies' and so on. Neither would he repeat himself in the clumsy way that Rouse does in 'I, who had set forth with Ponto to discover . . . *something* to . . . *shoot*' (sentence five) and 'my hitherto fixed resolution to *shoot something*' (sentence six); and in '*those* publications or indications by which the owners of property discourage *those* whose . . .'; and in 'for he *stood* as if petrified . . .' (sentence one) and 'The bristling hard hairs that *stood* up . . .' (sentence two). Such repetitions (one wonders if Rouse was himself aware that he had introduced them) are symptomatic of general *artistic* insensitivity, of a bad ear—the last thing James can be accused of.

Rouse's most serious misrepresentation is of James' diction. We have already noted how he overlooks entirely James' frequent dips into colloquial or even slangish registers, not only in dialogue but in straight narrative as well. He also misrepresents that aspect of James' diction which is more formal. Though his vocabulary is wide, and though he uses many polysyllabic words, James is not a devotee of inkhornisms, that is, really long and difficult words ('sixty-four dollar words' in the American term). His style is nothing like Johnson's, which delights in the sonorities and pomposities of long and arcane Latinate terminology. Rouse is quite wrong in introducing—as if they were widespread —words like 'contradictious', 'conterminate', 'disterminate', and 'supererogance'. He is also wrong to suggest that James frequently feeds the reader undigestible clumps of polysyllabic terms like 'ratiocinating movements of Supposition', 'propitiate some polysyllabic deity', 'contradictious architectural overarching boughs', and so on. Nor is it particularly Jamesian to evoke the exotic and the antique, as 'Aztecs', 'Mexico', and 'Matterhorn' would suggest.

But more obvious than any of these details as measures of the successes of Beerbohm and failures of Rouse are the larger stylistic domains—the style of narrative structure and the style of content (for it can be argued successfully, I think, that content is a subject of stylistics: *what* a writer chooses to write about— at the literal and at the figurative levels—serves to characterize his work just as much as how he chooses to express it; Hemingway is stylistically characterized by the fact that he typically chooses as heroes soldiers, bullfighters, hunters, fishermen, and so on). Now the subject of 'The Guerdon' is clearly the kind that would have interested James—a delicate social situation, rich in psychological implication, involving graceful and distinguished 'types'. On the other hand, Mr. Jingle's tale couldn't be *intrinsically* less Jamesian: the very appearance of a dog is rare in James' fiction,[1]

---

[1] I recall only Stenterello, the toy poodle of Christina Light in *Roderick Hudson*.

and the idea of making one a character quite unthinkable. There *are* limits of appropriate content which a style can hope to embody: it is difficult to imagine the plot of *The Golden Bowl* being recounted in the style of Hemingway or Gertrude Stein, or, conversely, that of 'The Killers' in the style of Henry James.

As for narrative structure, I have already mentioned the subject of point of view, but it is worth analysing the matter in closer detail, since it looms so largely in James' theory of fiction. Beerbohm's choice of limited third-person narrator is obviously more correct than Rouse's uneasy first person. Rouse either never read James' (or Lubbock's) description of 'the method' or did so without understanding it. The treatment of point of view in 'The Guerdon' is exact. In each sentence, Stamfordham is the abiding 'central consciousness', though in typical Jamesian fashion, his mind is conceived of as a space filled with rather formally expressed propositions rather than fragmented Joycean sense-perceptions or the like. These are abstract but they are represented as almost palpable: they 'flick his cheek', they 'loom' or 'burst' for him. There is no attempt to avoid the responsibility of narrative interpretation, no attempt to represent the 'very' unalloyed words that passed through Stamfordham's mind. This is not stream-of-consciousness, but classical limited third-person narration, in which a narrator, though convert, is clearly evident. Indeed, if he weren't, there would be little chance for the important effects of irony—so characteristically Jamesian.

The wavering first-person mode of 'The Enchanted Copse', on the other hand, could not have been more poorly chosen. James himself expressly dismissed the first person as 'a form foredoomed to looseness', representative of 'the darkest abyss of romance'; he referred almost contemptuously to 'the large ease of "autobiography" ' with its 'double privilege of subject and object'.[1] Of course if one argues that 'I' in Rouse's tale is witness

---

[1] See the preface to the New York edition of *The Ambassadors*, as reprinted in *The Art of the Novel*, ed. R. P. Blackmur (New York, 1934), pp. 320–1; and Blackmur's remarks on the subject in his 'Introduction', pp. xxix and xxx.

rather than protagonist (as in Fitzgerald's *The Great Gatsby*), the narrative can be defended against this charge, since the object is Ponto and the subject his master. But then another essential Jamesian narrative feature is precluded, namely our *immediate* access to the protagonist's mind, our sense of learning each thought the very moment that it is registered. Thus sentences like 'that this so sagacious creature should . . . stand petrified gazing at something hidden from me and undisclosed . . .' and 'where from a calculation of the angle of the sagacious creature's gaze I inferred that as likely to be situated, which had so remarkably and inexplicably attracted his attention' are not normally to be found in the later Jamesian style. Rather we learn what the hero perceives at the moment that he perceives it, not earlier nor later, and not by deduction, although, of course, the initial stages of the perception may be unclear or even inaccurate. But in that case we *share* the unclarity or inaccuracy with him; and the covert narrator does not intercede unduly.

Rouse's parody, in a way, is not a narrative at all, since the whole incident serves only to exemplify a thesis expressly spelled out in the last sentence, namely 'you should keep dogs, they are fine creatures of surprising instinct, and I once had one myself'. And James' fiction never argues a thesis; it is too concerned with showing how the world *is* to bother with how it should be.